International Benchmarks for Academic Library Use of Bibliometrics

ISBN: 978-1-57440-318-3
Library of Congress Control Number: 2014957625
© 2014 Primary Research Group Inc.

Table of Contents

THE QUESTIONNAIRE 11
SURVEY PARTICIPANTS 16
SUMMARY OF MAIN FINDINGS...17
    Use of Various Citation Indices & Tools: Web of Science 17
    Use of Various Citation Indices & Tools: Scopus Citation Index 17
    Use of Various Citation Indices & Tools: JSTOR..17
    Use of Various Citation Indices & Tools: Google Scholar...17
    Use of Various Citation Indices & Tools: Journal Citation Reports.............................17
    Use of Various Citation Indices & Tools: Use of Other Tools Not Previously Mentioned .18
    How Heavily Used is the Scimago Journal Ranking System at your Institution?.................18
    Trends in the Funding of Bibliometrics Research..18
    The Library Bibliometrics Staff...18
    Prospects for the Funding of Bibliometrics Staff and Services over the Next Few Years..19
    Self-Evaluation of Bibliometrics Services 19
    Demand for Bibliometrics Services Over the Past Two Years..19
    Source of Demand for Bibliometrics Services..20
    Experience of Pressure to Alter Methodologies to Generate Favorable Evaluations 20
    Use of Bibliometrics in Tenure Decisions 20
    The Role of the Library in Tracking International Scholarly Collaboration.................20
    Use of Altmetrics 21
    Evaluation of Altmetrics Methods 21
    Library Staff Time Spent on Bibliometrics 21
    Production of Bibliometrics Reports When Requested by Faculty or Administration.......21
    Production of Bibliometrics Reports in Specific Fields at Regular Intervals.................22
    Production of Bibliometrics Reports in Library Science 22
    Librarian Participation in Studies of Scholarly Output "Return on Investment"..................22
    How Libraries Promote Their Bibliometrics Capabilities and Services.........................22
    Advice to Peers...23
Table 1.1 Is your college public or private? 24
Table 1.2 Is your college public or private? Broken out by Country..................................24
Table 1.3 Is your college public or private? Broken out by Annual Tuition Level 24
Table 1.4 Is your college public or private? Broken out by FTE Student Enrollment 24
Table 1.5 Is your college public or private? Broken out by Carnegie Class 25
Table 2.1 What is the annual tuition ($) of your college prior to any financial aid or
deductions and excluding room and board? 26
Table 2.2 What is the annual tuition ($) of your college prior to any financial aid or
deductions and excluding room and board? Broken out by Country.......................................26
Table 2.3 What is the annual tuition ($) of your college prior to any financial aid or
deductions and excluding room and board? Broken out by Type of College.............................26
Table 2.4 What is the annual tuition ($) of your college prior to any financial aid or
deductions and excluding room and board? Broken out by FTE Student Enrollment............27

Table 2.5 What is the annual tuition ($) of your college prior to any financial aid or deductions and excluding room and board? Broken out by Carnegie Class 27
Table 3.1 What is the full time equivalent student enrollment at your institution? 28
Table 3.2 What is the full time equivalent student enrollment at your institution? Broken out by Country 28
Table 3.3 What is the full time equivalent student enrollment at your institution? Broken out by Type of College 28
Table 3.4 What is the full time equivalent student enrollment at your institution? Broken out by Annual Tuition Level 28
Table 3.5 What is the full time equivalent student enrollment at your institution? Broken out by Carnegie Class 29
Table 4.1 Your college might best be described as: 30
Table 4.2 Your college might best be described as: Broken out by Country 30
Table 4.3 Your college might best be described as: Broken out by Type of College 30
Table 4.4 Your college might best be described as: Broken out by Annual Tuition Level 30
Table 4.5 Your college might best be described as: Broken out by FTE Student Enrollment 31
Table 5 Which of the following citation indices does your library use in bibliometrics? 32
Table 5.1.1 Does your library use the Web of Science citation indices in bibliometrics? ..32
Table 5.1.2 Does your library use the Web of Science citation indices in bibliometrics? Broken out by Country 32
Table 5.1.3 Does your library use the Web of Science citation indices in bibliometrics? Broken out by Type of College 32
Table 5.1.4 Does your library use the Web of Science citation indices in bibliometrics? Broken out by Annual Tuition Level 32
Table 5.1.5 Does your library use the Web of Science citation indices in bibliometrics? Broken out by FTE Student Enrollment 33
Table 5.1.6 Does your library use the Web of Science citation indices in bibliometrics? Broken out by Carnegie Class 33
Table 5.2.1 Does your library use the Scopus citation indices in bibliometrics? 34
Table 5.2.2 Does your library use the Scopus citation indices in bibliometrics? Broken out by Country 34
Table 5.2.3 Does your library use the Scopus citation indices in bibliometrics? Broken out by Type of College 34
Table 5.2.4 Does your library use the Scopus citation indices in bibliometrics? Broken out by Annual Tuition Level 34
Table 5.2.5 Does your library use the Scopus citation indices in bibliometrics? Broken out by FTE Student Enrollment 34
Table 5.2.6 Does your library use the Scopus citation indices in bibliometrics? Broken out by Carnegie Class 35
Table 5.3.1 Does your library use JSTOR in bibliometrics? 36
Table 5.3.2 Does your library use JSTOR in bibliometrics? Broken out by Country 36
Table 5.3.3 Does your library use JSTOR in bibliometrics? Broken out by Type of College 36
Table 5.3.4 Does your library use JSTOR in bibliometrics? Broken out by Annual Tuition Level 36

Table 5.3.5 Does your library use JSTOR in bibliometrics? Broken out by FTE Student Enrollment 36
Table 5.3.6 Does your library use JSTOR in bibliometrics? Broken out by Carnegie Class 37
Table 5.4.1 Does your library use Google Scholar in bibliometrics? 38
Table 5.4.2 Does your library use Google Scholar in bibliometrics? Broken out by Country 38
Table 5.4.3 Does your library use Google Scholar in bibliometrics? Broken out by Type of College 38
Table 5.4.4 Does your library use Google Scholar in bibliometrics? Broken out by Annual Tuition Level 38
Table 5.4.5 Does your library use Google Scholar in bibliometrics? Broken out by FTE Student Enrollment 38
Table 5.4.6 Does your library use Google Scholar in bibliometrics? Broken out by Carnegie Class 39
Table 5.5.1 Does your library use Journal Citation Reports citation indices in bibliometrics? 40
Table 5.5.2 Does your library use Journal Citation Reports citation indices in bibliometrics? Broken out by Country 40
Table 5.5.3 Does your library use Journal Citation Reports citation indices in bibliometrics? Broken out by Type of College 40
Table 5.5.4 Does your library use Journal Citation Reports citation indices in bibliometrics? Broken out by Annual Tuition Level 40
Table 5.5.5 Does your library use Journal Citation Reports citation indices in bibliometrics? Broken out by FTE Student Enrollment 40
Table 5.5.6 Does your library use Journal Citation Reports citation indices in bibliometrics? Broken out by Carnegie Class 41
Does your library use other citation indices in bibliometrics? 42
Discuss your experience with Google Scholar as a citation analysis tool. 43
Table 6.1 How heavily used is the SciMago Journal Ranking system at your institution? 45
Table 6.2 How heavily used is the SciMago Journal Ranking system at your institution? Broken out by Country 45
Table 6.3 How heavily used is the SciMago Journal Ranking system at your institution? Broken out by Type of College 45
Table 6.4 How heavily used is the SciMago Journal Ranking system at your institution? Broken out by Annual Tuition Level 46
Table 6.5 How heavily used is the SciMago Journal Ranking system at your institution? Broken out by FTE Student Enrollment 46
Table 6.6 How heavily used is the SciMago Journal Ranking system at your institution? Broken out by Carnegie Class 46
Table 7.1 Over the Past three years, how has funding for bibliometrics research, staff and services at your library changed? 47
Table 7.2 Over the Past three years, how has funding for bibliometrics research, staff and services at your library changed? Broken out by Country 47
Table 7.3 Over the Past three years, how has funding for bibliometrics research, staff and services at your library changed? Broken out by Type of College 47

Table 7.4 Over the Past three years, how has funding for bibliometrics research, staff and services at your library changed? Broken out by Annual Tuition Level 48
Table 7.5 Over the Past three years, how has funding for bibliometrics research, staff and services at your library changed? Broken out by FTE Student Enrollment 48
Table 7.6 Over the Past three years, how has funding for bibliometrics research, staff and services at your library changed?: Broken out by Carnegie Class 49
Table 8.1 Which phrase best describes how your library staffs its bibliometrics services?.50
Table 8.2 Which phrase best describes how your library staffs its bibliometrics services? Broken out by Country 50
Table 8.3 Which phrase best describes how your library staffs its bibliometrics services? Broken out by Type of College 51
Table 8.4 Which phrase best describes how your library staffs its bibliometrics services? Broken out by Annual Tuition Level 51
Table 8.5 Which phrase best describes how your library staffs its bibliometrics services? Broken out by FTE Student Enrollment 52
Table 8.6 Which phrase best describes how your library staffs its bibliometrics services? Broken out by Carnegie Class 52
Table 9.1 What is the outlook for funding at your library for bibliometrics staff and services over the next few years?...53
Table 9.2 What is the outlook for funding at your library for bibliometrics staff and services over the next few years? Broken out by Country 53
Table 9.3 What is the outlook for funding at your library for bibliometrics staff and services over the next few years? Broken out by Type of College 53
Table 9.4 What is the outlook for funding at your library for bibliometrics staff and services over the next few years? Broken out by Annual Tuition Level 54
Table 9.5 What is the outlook for funding at your library for bibliometrics staff and services over the next few years? Broken out by FTE Student Enrollment 54
Table 9.6 What is the outlook for Funding at your library for bibliometrics staff and services over the next few years? Broken out by Carnegie Class 55
Table 10.1 What do you think of the bibliometrics capabilities of your own library or department of library science?..56
Table 10.2 What do you think of the bibliometrics capabilities of your own library or department of library science? Broken out by Country 56
Table 10.3 What do you think of the bibliometrics capabilities of your own library or department of library science? Broken out by Type of College...56
Table 10.4 What do you think of the bibliometrics capabilities of your own library or department of library science? Broken out by Annual Tuition Level 56
Table 10.5 What do you think of the bibliometrics capabilities of your own library or department of library science? Broken out by FTE Student Enrollment...57
Table 10.6 What do you think of the bibliometrics capabilities of your own library or department of library science? Broken out by Carnegie Class 57
Table 11.1 Demand for bibliometrics services at your library in the past two years has:......58
Table 11.2 Demand for bibliometrics services at your library in the past two years has: Broken out by Country..58
Table 11.3 Demand for bibliometrics services at your library in the past two years has: Broken out by Type of College...58

Table 11.4 Demand for bibliometrics services at your library in the past two years has: Broken out by Annual Tuition Level...59

Table 11.5 Demand for bibliometrics services at your library in the past two years has: Broken out by FTE Student Enrollment...59

Table 11.6 Demand for bibliometrics services at your library in the past two years has: Broken out by Carnegie Class 60

Which academic or administrative departments request the most assistance for bibliometrics services?...61

As a general average, how would you rate the skill of your college's faculty in developing, understanding and using bibliometrics evaluations? 62

Table 12.1 Have you or those working with you in your bibliometrics services ever felt pressure to alter methodologies to produce evaluations or results that may lead to more favorable evaluations of a colleges, department or individual faculty member's scholarly output?...63

Table 12.2 Have you or those working with you in your bibliometrics services ever felt pressure to alter methodologies to produce evaluations or results that may lead to more favorable evaluations of a colleges, department or individual faculty member's scholarly output? Broken out by Country 63

Table 12.3 Have you or those working with you in your bibliometrics services ever felt pressure to alter methodologies to produce evaluations or results that may lead to more favorable evaluations of a colleges, department or individual faculty member's scholarly output? Broken out by Type of College 63

Table 12.4 Have you or those working with you in your bibliometrics services ever felt pressure to alter methodologies to produce evaluations or results that may lead to more favorable evaluations of a colleges, department or individual faculty member's scholarly output? Broken out by Annual Tuition Level 64

Table 12.5 Have you or those working with you in your bibliometrics services ever felt pressure to alter methodologies to produce evaluations or results that may lead to more favorable evaluations of a colleges, department or individual faculty member's scholarly output? Broken out by FTE Student Enrollment...64

Table 12.6 Have you or those working with you in your bibliometrics services ever felt pressure to alter methodologies to produce evaluations or results that may lead to more favorable evaluations of a colleges, department or individual faculty member's scholarly output? Broken out by Carnegie Class...64

Table 13.1 To the best of your knowledge do any departments of your college require some form of bibliometrics analysis be done in tenure decision making or hiring decisions?........65

Table 13.2 To the best of your knowledge do any departments of your college require some form of bibliometrics analysis be done in tenure decision making or hiring decisions? Broken out by Country..65

Table 13.3 To the best of your knowledge do any departments of your college require some form of bibliometrics analysis be done in tenure decision making or hiring decisions? Broken out by Type of College..65

Table 13.4 To the best of your knowledge do any departments of your college require some form of bibliometrics analysis be done in tenure decision making or hiring decisions? Broken out by Annual Tuition Level...66

Table 13.5 To the best of your knowledge do any departments of your college require some form of bibliometrics analysis be done in tenure decision making or hiring decisions? Broken out by FTE Student Enrollment...66

Table 13.6 To the best of your knowledge do any departments of your college require some form of bibliometrics analysis be done in tenure decision making or hiring decisions? Broken out by Carnegie Class 66

Describe what role if any the academic library plays in providing bibliometrics services during the tenure review process at different departments of your institution. 67

Describe the library's role, if any, in advising your institution's office of research grants, technology licensing or other divisions about their use of bibliometrics and other tools in measuring the impact of scholarly output...68

Table 14.1 Does the library play any role in tracking collaboration networks of scholars in different subjects and countries to measure trends in collaboration between countries, institutions or even academic disciplines?...69

Table 14.2 Does the library play any role in tracking collaboration networks of scholars in different subjects and countries to measure trends in collaboration between countries, institutions or even academic disciplines? Broken out by Country...69

Table 14.3 Does the library play any role in tracking collaboration networks of scholars in different subjects and countries to measure trends in collaboration between countries, institutions or even academic disciplines? Broken out by Type of College.................................69

Table 14.4 Does the library play any role in tracking collaboration networks of scholars in different subjects and countries to measure trends in collaboration between countries, institutions or even academic disciplines? Broken out by Annual Tuition Level.......................70

Table 14.5 Does the library play any role in tracking collaboration networks of scholars in different subjects and countries to measure trends in collaboration between countries, institutions or even academic disciplines? Broken out by FTE Student Enrollment...............70

Table 14.6 Does the library play any role in tracking collaboration networks of scholars in different subjects and countries to measure trends in collaboration between countries, institutions or even academic disciplines? Broken out by Carnegie Class................................70

If the library plays any role in tracking collaboration networks of scholars in different subjects and countries to measure trends in collaboration between countries, institutions or even academic disciplines, what is that role?...71

What efforts has your library made in providing alternatives to traditional biometric techniques, alternatives which are often described under the banner "altmetrics"? 72

Table 15.1 How much confidence do you have that altmetric methods have already or will become reliable and competitive means of evaluating scholarly output similar to traditional bibliometrics methods? 74

Table 15.2 How much confidence do you have that altmetric methods have already or will become reliable and competitive means of evaluating scholarly output similar to traditional bibliometrics methods? Broken out by Country...74

Table 15.3 How much confidence do you have that altmetric methods have already or will become reliable and competitive means of evaluating scholarly output similar to traditional bibliometrics methods? Broken out by Type of College 75

Table 15.4 How much confidence do you have that altmetric methods have already or will become reliable and competitive means of evaluating scholarly output similar to traditional bibliometrics methods? Broken out by Annual Tuition Level 75

Table 15.5 How much confidence do you have that altmetric methods have already or will become reliable and competitive means of evaluating scholarly output similar to traditional bibliometrics methods? Broken out by FTE Student Enrollment 76

Table 15.6 How much confidence do you have that altmetric methods have already or will become reliable and competitive means of evaluating scholarly output similar to traditional bibliometrics methods? Broken out by Carnegie Class 76

Table 16.1 How much annual staff time in hours would you say that your library staff expends in teaching faculty about publication lists and rankings, citation impact tools and methods, and other bibliometrics and citation analysis processes and procedures? (one person working full time would be about 1850 hours) 77

Table 16.2 How much annual staff time in hours would you say that your library staff expends in teaching faculty about publication lists and rankings, citation impact tools and methods, and other bibliometrics and citation analysis processes and procedures? (One person working full time would be about 1850 hours) Broken out by Country 77

Table 16.3 How much annual staff time in hours would you say that your library staff expends in teaching faculty about publication lists and rankings, citation impact tools and methods, and other bibliometrics and citation analysis processes and procedures? (One person working full time would be about 1850 hours) Broken out by Type of College 78

Table 16.4 How much annual staff time in hours would you say that your library staff expends in teaching faculty about publication lists and rankings, citation impact tools and methods, and other bibliometrics and citation analysis processes and procedures? (One person working full time would be about 1850 hours) Broken out by Annual Tuition Level 78

Table 16.5 How much annual staff time in hours would you say that your library staff expends in teaching faculty about publication lists and rankings, citation impact tools and methods, and other bibliometrics and citation analysis processes and procedures? (One person working full time would be about 1850 hours) Broken out by FTE Student Enrollment 79

Table 16.6 How much annual staff time in hours would you say that your library staff expends in teaching faculty about publication lists and rankings, citation impact tools and methods, and other bibliometrics and citation analysis processes and procedures? (One person working full time would be about 1850 hours) Broken out by Carnegie Class 79

Table 17 Does the library produce any of the following bibliometrics reports? 80

Table 17.1.1 Does the library produce ad hoc bibliometrics reports when requested by faculty or administration? 80

Table 17.1.2 Does the library produce ad hoc bibliometrics reports when requested by faculty or administration? Broken out by Country 80

Table 17.1.3 Does the library produce ad hoc bibliometrics reports when requested by faculty or administration? Broken out by Type of College 80

Table 17.1.4 Does the library produce ad hoc bibliometrics reports when requested by faculty or administration? Broken out by Annual Tuition Level 80

Table 17.1.5 Does the library produce ad hoc bibliometrics reports when requested by faculty or administration? Broken out by FTE Student Enrollment 81

Table 17.1.6 Does the library produce ad hoc bibliometrics reports when requested by faculty or administration? Broken out by Carnegie Class 81

Table 17.2.1 Does the library produce reports in specific fields produced at regular and expected intervals? 82
Table 17.2.2 Does the library produce reports in specific fields produced at regular and expected intervals? Broken out by Country..82
Table 17.2.3 Does the library produce reports in specific fields produced at regular and expected intervals? Broken out by Type of College 82
Table 17.2.4 Does the library produce reports in specific fields produced at regular and expected intervals? Broken out by Annual Tuition Level 82
Table 17.2.5 Does the library produce reports in specific fields produced at regular and expected intervals? Broken out by FTE Student Enrollment 82
Table 17.2.6 Does the library produce reports in specific fields produced at regular and expected intervals? Broken out by Carnegie Class 83
Table 17.3.1 Does the library produce bibliometrics reports about scholarly output of library personnel or faculty?..84
Table 17.3.2 Does the library produce bibliometrics reports about scholarly output of library personnel or faculty? Broken out by Country 84
Table 17.3.3 Does the library produce bibliometrics reports about scholarly output of library personnel or faculty? Broken out by Type of College................................84
Table 17.3.4 Does the library produce bibliometrics reports about scholarly output of library personnel or faculty? Broken out by Annual Tuition Level.......................84
Table 17.3.5 Does the library produce bibliometrics reports about scholarly output of library personnel or faculty? Broken out by FTE Student Enrollment.................84
Table 17.3.6 Does the library produce bibliometrics reports about scholarly output of library personnel or faculty? Broken out by Carnegie Class.................................85
All forms of bibliometrics analysis have some limitations. Some citations of an article may point out that the article is unexceptional or erroneous; major bibliometrics tools indices only cover a certain range of publications, etc. and may create a misleading picture. Has your library devised a "cocktail" or master formula to minimize the disadvantages of any one approach and to insure breadth and reliability, at least to the extent that this is possible. If so describe the methodologies that your library has developed. (Also identify yourself if you wish for this question)...86
Table 18.1 Has the library been asked to participate in studies through which a kind of scholarly output "return on investment" might be calculated by comparing dollars invested in research to the resulting scholarly output?..88
If you have participated in any studies through which the link between sums of money or time invested and scholarly output are linked then please describe one of these projects..88
Table 19.1 Does the library manage a bibliometrics database that periodically measures the likely impact of publications from the college's faculty?...89
Table 19.2 Does the library manage a bibliometrics database that periodically measures the likely impact of publications from the college's faculty? Broken out by Country 89
Table 19.3 Does the library manage a bibliometrics database that periodically measures the likely impact of publications from the college's faculty? Broken out by Type of College.......89
Table 19.4 Does the library manage a bibliometrics database that periodically measures the likely impact of publications from the college's faculty? Broken out by Annual Tuition Level 90

Table 19.5 Does the library manage a bibliometrics database that periodically measures the likely impact of publications from the college's faculty? Broken out by FTE Student Enrollment 90

Table 19.6 Does the library manage a bibliometrics database that periodically measures the likely impact of publications from the college's faculty? Broken out by Carnegie Class 90

If yes how controversial is this database in your institution? What are the politics involved in challenging it? Is there some form of appeal mechanism? 91

How does the library promote its bibliometrics and citation analysis services? 92

What advice can you offer to your peers on the best way to establish, promote and manage a bibliometrics service at their college or university? 93

THE QUESTIONNAIRE

Introductory Information

1. Please give us the following contact information

    A. Name
    B. Institution
    C. Work Title
    D. Country
    E. Email Address

2. Is your college public or private?

    A. Public
    B. Private

3. What is the annual tuition of your college prior to any financial aid or deductions and excluding room and board?

4. What is the full time equivalent student enrollment at your institution?

5. Your college might best be described as:

    A. Community College
    B. 4Year College
    C. MA/PHD Granting
    D. Research University

Citation Indexes

6. Which of the following citation indices does your library use in bibliometrics?

    A. Web of Science
    B. Scopus
    C. JSTOR
    D. Google Scholar
    E. Journal Citation Reports
    F. Other (please specify)

7. Discuss your experience with Google Scholar as a citation analysis tool.

8. How heavily used is the SciMago Journal Ranking system at your institution?

    A. Unaware of it
    B. Not Used Much
    C. Used Somewhat
    D. Used a Lot
    E. Used a Great Deal

Official Staff and Funding

9. Over the Past three years, funding for bibliometrics research, staff and services at your library has:

    A. Diminished Significantly
    B. Diminished
    C. Remained Approximately the Same
    D. Increased
    E. Increased Significantly

10. Which phrase best describes how your library staffs its bibliometrics services?

    A. We have a dedicated staff of bibliometrics specialists
    B. We have on real specialist and others who work part time on the issue
    C. It is one specialty among others for a number of librarians but no specific staff or position
    D. Honestly we do not have too much expertize in this area

11. Funding at your library for bibliometrics staff and services over the next few years is:

    A. Likely to Diminish Significantly
    B. Likely to Diminish
    C. Likely to Remain Approximately the Same
    D. Likely to Increase

    E. Likely to Increase Significantly

12. What do you think of the bibliometrics capabilities of your own library or department of library science?

    F. Excellent
    G. Good
    H. Acceptable
    I. Poor

Demand for Bibliometrics Services

13. Demand for bibliometrics services at your library in the past two years has:

    A. Fallen considerably
    B. Fallen somewhat
    C. Remained about the same
    D. Increased somewhat
    E. Increased considerably

14. Which academic or administrative departments request the most assistance for bibliometrics services?

15. As a general average, how would you rate the skill of your college's faculty in developing, understanding and using bibliometrics evaluations?

16. Have you or those working with you in your bibliometrics services ever felt pressure to alter methodologies to produce evaluations or results that may lead to more favorable evaluations of a colleges, department or individual faculty member's scholarly output?

    A. Yes
    B. No

17. To the best of your knowledge do any departments of your college require some form of bibliometrics analysis be done in tenure decision making or hiring decisions?

    A. Yes
    B. No
    C. Do not really know

Range of Effort in Bibliometrics

18. Describe what role if any the academic library plays in providing bibliometrics services during the tenure review process at different departments of your institution.

19. Describe the library's role, if any, in advising your institution's office of research grants, technology licensing or other divisions about their use of bibliometrics and other tools in measuring the impact of scholarly output.

20. Does the library play any role in tracking collaboration networks of scholars in different subjects and countries to measure trends in collaboration between countries, institutions or even academic disciplines?

    A. Yes
    B. No

21. If so what is that role?

Altmetrics

22. What efforts has your library made in providing alternatives to traditional biometric techniques, alternatives which are often described under the banner "altmetrics"?

23. How much confidence do you have that altmetric methods have already or will become reliable and competitive means of evaluating scholarly output similar to traditional bibliometrics methods?

    A. They are superior to and will eventually supplant traditional methods
    B. They are already important and competitive with traditional methods
    C. They are an adjunct and useful but subordinate methodology
    D. They are more or less a fad and don't really add much
    E. They are misleading and more or less a waste of time

Regular Staff Responsibilities in Bibliometrics/Citation Analysis

24. How much annual staff time in hours would you say that your library staff expends in teaching faculty about publication lists and rankings, citation impact tools and methods, and other bibliometrics and citation analysis processes and procedures? (one person working full time would be about 1850 hours)

25. Does the library produce any of the following:

    A. Ad hoc bibliometrics reports when requested by faculty or administration
    B. Reports in specific fields produced at regular and expected intervals
    C. Bibliometrics reports about scholarly output of library personnel or faculty

26. All forms of bibliometrics analysis have some limitations. Some citations of an article may point out that the article is unexceptional or erroneous; major bibliometrics tools indices only cover a certain range of publications, etc. and may create a misleading picture. Has your library devised a "cocktail" or master formula to minimize the disadvantages of any one approach and to insure breadth and reliability, at least to the extent that this is possible. If so describe the methodologies that your library has developed. (Also identify yourself if you wish for this question).

Bibliometrics and Scholarly Productivity

27. Has the library been asked to participate in studies through which a kind of scholarly output "return on investment" might be calculated by comparing dollars invested in research to the resulting scholarly output?

    A. Yes
    B. No

28. If you have participated in any studies through which the link between sums of money or time invested and scholarly output are linked then please describe one of these projects.

Management of a Bibliometrics Database

29. Does the library manage a bibliometrics database that periodically measures the likely impact of publications from the college's faculty?

    A. Yes
    B. No

30. If yes how controversial is this database in your institution? What are the politics involved in challenging it? Is there some form of appeal mechanism?

31. How does the library promote its bibliometrics and citation analysis services?

Advice

32. What advice can you offer to your peers on the best way to establish, promote and manage a bibliometrics service at their college or university?

SURVEY PARTICIPANTS

Aberystwyth University
American University
Carnegie Mellon University
Corban University
Cornell University (State University of NY)
Durban University of Technology
Forschungszentrum Jülich
James Cook University
Leeds Beckett University
London School of Economics
London School of Hygiene & Tropical Medicine
Loughborough University
Mississippi State University
Northern Illinois University
Open University
SUNY University at Buffalo
Texas Tech University Lubock
The Rockefeller University
Technische Universität München
University College Dublin
University of Bradford
University of Cambridge
University of Lethbridge
University of Limerick
University of Memphis
University of Newcastle
University of Seville
University of Waterloo Library
University of Wisconsin - Eau Claire
Wageningen University and Research Centre

SUMMARY OF MAIN FINDINGS

Use of Various Citation Indices & Tools: Web of Science

We asked the colleges in the sample, which of the following citation indices does their library uses in bibliometrics. First we asked about use of the Web of Science, citation index; it was used by 87.10% of the libraries in the sample. All libraries in the UK or Ireland, and all libraries in countries other than the United States, the UK and Ireland use Web of Science; two thirds of the libraries in the USA used Web of Science. Close to 89% of public colleges used it while we 75% of private colleges did.

Use of Various Citation Indices & Tools: Scopus Citation Index

Next we asked about the Scopus citation index. Approximately 71% of the libraries in the sample use Scopus in their bibliometrics approach. Once again, libraries in the USA were the least likely to use it; only a little more than 58% of US libraries did so. 100% of private college libraries use it, but only 66.67% of public college libraries did.

Use of Various Citation Indices & Tools: JSTOR

Only 29% of the libraries in this in the sample used the JSTOR citation index in their bibliometrics approach. A third of libraries in the USA use it while only 10% of those in the UK and Ireland did so.   Also, the higher the level of student enrollment, the greater the use of JSTOR as a bibliometrics tool.

Use of Various Citation Indices & Tools: Google Scholar

Nearly 81% of the libraries in the sample use Google scholar in bibliometrics.

Use of Various Citation Indices & Tools: Journal Citation Reports

37.42% of libraries in the sample use Journal Citation Reports in their bibliometrics approach. Its use was most common in the UK and Ireland where 90% of the libraries in the sample used it.

Use of Various Citation Indices & Tools: Use of Other Tools Not Previously Mentioned
Other tools and indicia used by the libraries in the sample include altmetrics.com, inCite; Publish or Perish, Scimago, essential science indicators and Leiden.

How Heavily Used is the Scimago Journal Ranking System at your Institution?

We asked how heavily used is the Scimago Journal Ranking System at your institution? We gave 5 possible answers to this multiple-choice question: 1 – unaware of it; 2 – do not use much; 3 – use somewhat; 4 – used a lot; 5 – used a great deal. 25.81% of those sampled said that they were unaware of the Scimago journal ranking system. Another 29% said it was not used much, while 38.71% said it was used somewhat and 3.23% said it was used a lot. None said it was used a great deal. Its use was heaviest in countries outside of the USA, UK and Ireland. Only in these countries, mostly European countries, was the Scimago journal ranking system used a lot. Its use was greatest in public universities; half of those in private colleges had never heard of it.

Trends in the Funding of Bibliometrics Research

We asked the libraries in the sample what had been the trend over the past 3 years for funding for bibliometrics research, staff and services at their library. We gave them 5 choices in this multiple-choice question; 1 – diminished significantly; 2 – diminished; 3 – remained approximately the same; 4 – increased; 5 – increased significantly. In general funding seems to be modestly increasing. For 3.23% it had diminished significantly and for another 9.8% it had diminished. For a plurality of 45.16%, it had remained approximately the same. However, it increased for 25.81% and increased significantly for 9.68%. The ratio of those libraries that saw increased funding to those that saw diminished funding was approximately 3 to 1. Almost all of those increasing funding were libraries in the UK, Ireland, Continental Europe and other countries other than the United States. In the United States funding increased for only 8.33% of survey participants and remained the same for two thirds of them. But in the UK and Ireland funding increased for 50% of survey participants and it increased for 55.5% in countries other than the USA, UK and Ireland. 44% of research universities in the sample experienced an increase or a significant increase in funding over the past 3 years.

The Library Bibliometrics Staff

We gave the libraries in the sample a choice of 4 phrases and asked which one best describes how the library staffs its bibliometrics services. The 4 choices were: 1 – We have a dedicated staff of bibliometrics specialists; 2 – we have one specialist, and others who work part-time on the issue; 3 – it is one specialty among others for a number of librarians but we have no specific staff or position; 4 -- Honestly we do not have too much expertise in this area. Only 6.45% of the libraries in the sample have a dedicated staff of bibliometrics specialists. Another 22.58% have one real specialist, and others who work part-time on the issue; 54.84% say it is a specialty among others for a number of librarians but there is no specific staff position. 12.9% say that honestly they don't have much expertise in this area.

Prospects for the Funding of Bibliometrics Staff and Services over the Next Few Years

We asked the libraries in the sample what the prospects were for funding bibliometrics staff and services at their library over the next few years. Once again, we gave them 5 choices to this multiple-choice question: 1 -- likely to diminish significantly; 2 – likely to diminish; 3 – likely to remain approximately the same; 4 – likely to increase; 5 – likely to increase significantly. For 51.61% of the libraries in the sample their funding was likely to remain the same; but for 3.23% it was likely to diminish significantly, while for 6.45% it was likely to diminish. However, for 35.48% it was likely to increase, although is not likely to increase significantly for any library in the sample. Nonetheless, the ratio of libraries likely to experience an increase in funding for bibliometrics staff and services to those likely to experience diminishment of funding for bibliometrics staff and services was more than 3.5 to 1. The most optimistic universities were those in the "all other" category, mostly from continental Europe. 55.56% of them said that they were likely to have increased funding for bibliometrics staff and services over the next few years; likewise the funding outlook was also very good for libraries from the UK and Ireland, of which 40% thought that they would experience increased funding. However, in the United States, only 16.67% felt that they would experience increase funding over the next few years.

Self-Evaluation of Bibliometrics Services

We asked the libraries in the sample what they think of the bibliometrics capabilities of their own library or Dept. of library science. We gave them four choices: excellent, good, acceptable and poor. Only 6.45% chose excellent and 25.81% good; 51.61% chose acceptable and 16.13% poor. Research universities thought a little more highly of their skills than did other types of colleges; a third of them considered their capabilities good.

Demand for Bibliometrics Services Over the Past Two Years

We asked the libraries in the sample what happened to demand for bibliometrics services at their library over the past 2 years. We gave them 5 choices in this multiple-choice question; 1 – fallen considerably; 2 – fallen somewhat; 3 – remained about the same; 4 – increased somewhat; 5 – increased considerably. None said that it had fallen considerably nor somewhat; 25.81% said it had remained about the same, while it increased somewhat for 48.39% and increased considerably for 22.58%.

Increases in demand were particularly strong in the UK/Ireland where it had increased somewhat or considerably for all survey participants from these countries. Demand growth was also fast for the rest of the world (predominantly continental Europe) increasing for nearly 78% of those sampled. It was also particularly strong among research universities for which nearly 90% had experienced increased demand for bibliometrics services within the past two years.

Source of Demand for Bibliometrics Services

We asked where the demand for bibliometrics services was coming from. A good deal was coming from individual faculty members; other sources of demand are research and planning offices, Boards of Directors, assessment staff, research managers and department heads and offices of institutional planning. In addition, on a subject basis, the most active areas seem to be medicine and life sciences, engineering and computer science, among others.

Experience of Pressure to Alter Methodologies to Generate Favorable Evaluations

We asked the librarians sampled if in their bibliometrics services had they ever felt pressure to alter methodologies to produce evaluations or results that may lead to more favorable evaluations of a colleges, department or individual faculty member's scholarly output? Only 6.45% said yes and 3.23% did not answer the question; more than 90% said no. All of the "yes" answers were in smaller colleges with less than 11,000 students.

Use of Bibliometrics in Tenure Decisions

We also asked if to the best of your knowledge do any departments of your college require some form of bibliometrics analysis be done in tenure decision making or hiring decisions? 51.61% said yes and 22.58% no while the same percentage did not really know. Colleges in the "all other" category, once again mostly from continental Europe, were the most likely to say that bibliometrics analysis was required in tenure or hiring decisions.

The Role of the Library in Tracking International Scholarly Collaboration

We asked: Does the library play any role in tracking collaboration networks of scholars in different subjects and countries to measure trends in collaboration between countries, institutions or even academic disciplines? 25% said yes, including 44.44% at research universities.

Then we asked what this role was precisely, if the library plays one in this process of tracing scholarly collaboration internationally. Roles differed significantly but we liked one library's response in particular: "We collaborate extensively with other institutions, particularly in the developing world and we use bibliometrics to track collaborations with key institutions and to track the top performing institutions within specific subject areas."

Use of Altmetrics

We asked the libraries in the sample what they were doing in altmetrics, alternative ways to analyze scholarly output and significance. Some of the applications and vehicles being used were: altmetrics.com, Plum Analytics, and Altmetrics.Explorer.

Evaluation of Altmetrics Methods

We asked librarians sampled how much confidence did they have that altmetrics methods have already or will become reliable and competitive means of evaluating scholarly output similar to traditional bibliometrics methods? We gave them five choices in this multiple choice question: 1) They are superior to and will eventually supplant traditional methods 2) They are already important and competitive with traditional methods; 3) They are an adjunct and useful but subordinate methodology; 4) They are more or less a fad and don't really add much; 5) They are misleading and more or less a waste of time.

None thought that they were superior to and will eventually supplant traditional methods while 32.26% thought that they were already important and competitive with traditional methods. A majority, 61.29%, believed that they are an adjunct and useful but subordinate methodology while 3.23% believed that they are more or less a fad and don't really add much. None believed that they are misleading and more or less a waste of time. All of the colleges that thought them already important were public colleges; no private college in the sample thought them anything other than an adjunct methodology. Also, colleges in the UK and Ireland were more likely than others to consider these techniques already important.

Library Staff Time Spent on Bibliometrics

We asked the sample of librarians: How much annual staff time in hours would you say that your library staff expends in teaching faculty about publication lists and rankings, citation impact tools and methods, and other bibliometrics and citation analysis processes and procedures?

The mean annual number of staff hours expended annually was about one fifth of a full time position – or 346.27 hours – though the median was just 90 hours. The range was 0 to 1850 hours. Libraries in the UK and Ireland were spending the most staff time, a mean of 539.44 hours vs only 160 for the US libraries in the sample. Research universities spent the most time, a mean of 458 staff hours.

Production of Bibliometrics Reports When Requested by Faculty or Administration

We asked if the library produced ad hoc bibliometrics reports when requested by faculty or administration. 64.52% of the libraries in the sample did so. Libraries in the UK/Ireland were the most likely to produce such reports and 90% of these sampled did so. Nearly 89% of research universities sampled produced these reports when requested by faculty or administration.

Production of Bibliometrics Reports in Specific Fields at Regular Intervals

Next we asked whether the library produces reports in specific fields at regular and expected intervals. Close to 26% of the libraries in the sample did so; about 39% of research universities did.

Production of Bibliometrics Reports in Library Science

We also asked if the library produces bibliometrics reports about the scholarly output of library personnel or faculty. 22.58% of the libraries sampled produced such reports; only 8.335 of the libraries in the USA did so.

Librarian Participation in Studies of Scholarly Output "Return on Investment"

We asked the libraries sampled if they had been asked to participate in studies through which a kind of scholarly output "return on investment" might be calculated by comparing dollars invested in research to the resulting scholarly output. No libraries in the sample have been asked to participate in any research of this kind.

We asked the libraries surveyed if they manage a bibliometrics database through which they periodically measure the likely impact of publications from the college's faculty? Only 6.45% did so; none were from the United States. All were public colleges. The experience of most seems to suggest a steep learning curve. One library discontinued its service; another cites low use. Still others say that results can be controversial and misleading. We particularly liked what one librarian wrote and reproduce it below:

> "Our research office manages this role. Issues that I know of are (1) many researchers do not feel that benchmarking their research against others in their School/College is appropriate because e.g. their specific area of research is poorly cited and (2) the average or median benchmarks create a lot of stress for researchers in high achieving Schools / Colleges because many that fall below these metrics are still doing quite well by national and international standards."

How Libraries Promote Their Bibliometrics Capabilities and Services

For the most part the libraries in the sample used relatively basic means to promote their bibliometrics capabilities to faculty and administration, including targeted emails, intranet and website pages, leaflets, reports, Twitter, blogs, workshops, seminars, presentations, and group and one on one training sessions. Some get exposure through library subject specialists and liaisons who bring word of the capabilities to faculty in their respective specializations.

Advice to Peers

We asked the sample what advice they could offer to their peers on the best way to establish, promote and manage a bibliometrics service at their college or university. Perhaps the most salient advice was to keep in touch with subject librarians and interested staff in academic departments to "evangelize" and spread interest. Others offered reference to information sources of use, and emphasized presentations.

Table 1.1 Is your college public or private?

	No Answer	Public	Private
Entire sample	0,00%	87,10%	12,90%

Table 1.2 Is your college public or private? Broken out by Country

Country	Public	Private
USA	66,67%	33,33%
UK / Ireland	100,00%	0,00%
All Other	100,00%	0,00%

Table 1.3 Is your college public or private? Broken out by Annual Tuition Level

Annual Tuition Level	Public	Private
less than $9000	100,00%	0,00%
$9000 - $14000	90,00%	10,00%
more than $14000	70,00%	30,00%

Table 1.4 Is your college public or private? Broken out by FTE Student Enrollment

FTE Student Enrollment	Public	Private
less than 11000	81,82%	18,18%
11000 - 22000	80,00%	20,00%
more than 22000	100,00%	0,00%

Table 1.5 Is your college public or private? Broken out by Carnegie Class

Carnegie Class	Public	Private
4-Year College	75,00%	25,00%
MA/PHD Granting	77,78%	22,22%
Research University	94,44%	5,56%

Table 2.1 What is the annual tuition ($) of your college prior to any financial aid or deductions and excluding room and board?

	Mean	Median	Minimum	Maximum
Entire sample	13158,45	13000,00	615,00	48030,00

Table 2.2 What is the annual tuition ($) of your college prior to any financial aid or deductions and excluding room and board? Broken out by Country

Country	Mean	Median	Minimum	Maximum
USA	18396,83	12500,00	7700,00	48030,00
UK / Ireland	12934,00	14089,50	5264,00	14410,00
All Other	6423,33	2622,00	615,00	18840,00

Table 2.3 What is the annual tuition ($) of your college prior to any financial aid or deductions and excluding room and board? Broken out by Type of College

Type of College	Mean	Median	Minimum	Maximum
Public	11267,56	11468,00	615,00	47286,00
Private	25922,00	21329,00	13000,00	48030,00

Table 2.4 What is the annual tuition ($) of your college prior to any financial aid or deductions and excluding room and board? Broken out by FTE Student Enrollment

FTE Student Enrollment	Mean	Median	Minimum	Maximum
less than 11000	11347,73	13000,00	1600,00	22000,00
11000 - 22000	19558,70	14410,00	615,00	48030,00
more than 22000	8750,00	8350,00	1279,00	15000,00

Table 2.5 What is the annual tuition ($) of your college prior to any financial aid or deductions and excluding room and board? Broken out by Carnegie Class

Carnegie Class	Mean	Median	Minimum	Maximum
4-Year College	10898,25	9516,50	2560,00	22000,00
MA/PHD Granting	14143,11	9000,00	615,00	48030,00
Research University	13168,39	13144,50	1600,00	47286,00

Table 3.1 What is the full time equivalent student enrollment at your institution?

	Mean	Median	Minimum	Maximum
Entire sample	24137,75	17000,00	200,00	200000,00

Table 3.2 What is the full time equivalent student enrollment at your institution? Broken out by Country

Country	Mean	Median	Minimum	Maximum
USA	16381,03	18500,00	200,00	35000,00
UK / Ireland	32839,80	13618,50	2439,00	200000,00
All Other	24811,11	19000,00	2000,00	70000,00

Table 3.3 What is the full time equivalent student enrollment at your institution? Broken out by Type of College

Type of College	Mean	Median	Minimum	Maximum
Public	26761,30	19000,00	2000,00	200000,00
Private	6428,85	6542,70	200,00	12430,00

Table 3.4 What is the full time equivalent student enrollment at your institution? Broken out by Annual Tuition Level

Annual Tuition Level	Mean	Median	Minimum	Maximum
less than $9000	38377,91	19000,00	2000,00	200000,00
$9000 - $14000	18110,10	20500,00	200,00	35000,00
more than $14000	14501,24	12157,70	1200,00	38000,00

Table 3.5 What is the full time equivalent student enrollment at your institution? Broken out by Carnegie Class

Carnegie Class	Mean	Median	Minimum	Maximum
4-Year College	74800,00	49000,00	1200,00	200000,00
MA/PHD Granting	19168,38	17000,00	8200,00	35000,00
Research University	15364,17	13618,50	200,00	38000,00

Table 4.1 Your college might best be described as:

	4-Year College	MA/PHD Granting	Research University
Entire sample	12,90%	29,03%	58,06%

Table 4.2 Your college might best be described as: Broken out by Country

Country	4-Year College	MA/PHD Granting	Research University
USA	8,33%	41,67%	50,00%
UK / Ireland	20,00%	0,00%	80,00%
All Other	11,11%	44,44%	44,44%

Table 4.3 Your college might best be described as: Broken out by Type of College

Type of College	4-Year College	MA/PHD Granting	Research University
Public	11,11%	25,93%	62,96%
Private	25,00%	50,00%	25,00%

Table 4.4 Your college might best be described as: Broken out by Annual Tuition Level

Annual Tuition Level	4Year College	MA/PHD Granting	Research University
less than $9000	18,18%	36,36%	45,45%
$9000 - $14000	10,00%	20,00%	70,00%
more than $14000	10,00%	30,00%	60,00%

Table 4.5 Your college might best be described as: Broken out by FTE Student Enrollment

FTE Student Enrollment	4-Year College	MA/PHD Granting	Research University
less than 11000	9,09%	9,09%	81,82%
11000 - 22000	0,00%	60,00%	40,00%
more than 22000	30,00%	20,00%	50,00%

Table 5 Which of the following citation indices does your library use in bibliometrics?

Table 5.1.1 Does your library use the Web of Science citation indices in bibliometrics?

	No Answer	Yes	No
Entire sample	0,00%	87,10%	12,90%

Table 5.1.2 Does your library use the Web of Science citation indices in bibliometrics? Broken out by Country

Country	Yes	No
USA	66,67%	33,33%
UK / Ireland	100,00%	0,00%
All Other	100,00%	0,00%

Table 5.1.3 Does your library use the Web of Science citation indices in bibliometrics? Broken out by Type of College

Type of College	Yes	No
Public	88,89%	11,11%
Private	75,00%	25,00%

Table 5.1.4 Does your library use the Web of Science citation indices in bibliometrics? Broken out by Annual Tuition Level

Annual Tuition Level	Yes	No
less than $9000	81,82%	18,18%
$9000 - $14000	90,00%	10,00%
more than $14000	90,00%	10,00%

Table 5.1.5 Does your library use the Web of Science citation indices in bibliometrics? Broken out by FTE Student Enrollment

FTE Student Enrollment	Yes	No
less than 11000	90,91%	9,09%
11000 - 22000	80,00%	20,00%
more than 22000	90,00%	10,00%

Table 5.1.6 Does your library use the Web of Science citation indices in bibliometrics? Broken out by Carnegie Class

Carnegie Class	Yés	No
4-Year College	75,00%	25,00%
MA/PHD Granting	88,89%	11,11%
Research University	88,89%	11,11%

Table 5.2.1 Does your library use the Scopus citation indices in bibliometrics?

	No Answer	Yes	No
Entire sample	0,00%	70,97%	29,03%

Table 5.2.2 Does your library use the Scopus citation indices in bibliometrics? Broken out by Country

Country	Yes	No
USA	58,33%	41,67%
UK / Ireland	80,00%	20,00%
All Other	77,78%	22,22%

Table 5.2.3 Does your library use the Scopus citation indices in bibliometrics? Broken out by Type of College

Type of College	Yes	No
Public	66,67%	33,33%
Private	100,00%	0,00%

Table 5.2.4 Does your library use the Scopus citation indices in bibliometrics? Broken out by Annual Tuition Level

Annual Tuition Level	Yes	No
less than $9000	54,55%	45,45%
$9000 - $14000	80,00%	20,00%
more than $14000	80,00%	20,00%

Table 5.2.5 Does your library use the Scopus citation indices in bibliometrics? Broken out by FTE Student Enrollment

FTE Student Enrollment	Yes	No
less than 11000	72,73%	27,27%
11000 - 22000	70,00%	30,00%
more than 22000	70,00%	30,00%

Table 5.2.6 Does your library use the Scopus citation indices in bibliometrics? Broken out by Carnegie Class

Carnegie Class	Yes	No
4-Year College	75,00%	25,00%
MA/PHD Granting	66,67%	33,33%
Research University	72,22%	27,78%

Table 5.3.1 Does your library use JSTOR in bibliometrics?

	No Answer	Yes	No
Entire sample	0,00%	29,03%	70,97%

Table 5.3.2 Does your library use JSTOR in bibliometrics? Broken out by Country

Country	Yes	No
USA	33,33%	66,67%
UK / Ireland	10,00%	90,00%
All Other	44,44%	55,56%

Table 5.3.3 Does your library use JSTOR in bibliometrics? Broken out by Type of College

Type of College	Yes	No
Public	29,63%	70,37%
Private	25,00%	75,00%

Table 5.3.4 Does your library use JSTOR in bibliometrics? Broken out by Annual Tuition Level

Annual Tuition Level	Yes	No
less than $9000	27,27%	72,73%
$9000 - $14000	40,00%	60,00%
more than $14000	20,00%	80,00%

Table 5.3.5 Does your library use JSTOR in bibliometrics? Broken out by FTE Student Enrollment

FTE Student Enrollment	Yes	No
less than 11000	9,09%	90,91%
11000 - 22000	30,00%	70,00%
more than 22000	50,00%	50,00%

Table 5.3.6 Does your library use JSTOR in bibliometrics? Broken out by Carnegie Class

Carnegie Class	Yes	No
4-Year College	25,00%	75,00%
MA/PHD Granting	33,33%	66,67%
Research University	27,78%	72,22%

Table 5.4.1 Does your library use Google Scholar in bibliometrics?

	No Answer	Yes	No
Entire sample	0,00%	80,65%	19,35%

Table 5.4.2 Does your library use Google Scholar in bibliometrics? Broken out by Country

Country	Yes	No
USA	75,00%	25,00%
UK / Ireland	90,00%	10,00%
All Other	77,78%	22,22%

Table 5.4.3 Does your library use Google Scholar in bibliometrics? Broken out by Type of College

Type of College	Yes	No
Public	81,48%	18,52%
Private	75,00%	25,00%

Table 5.4.4 Does your library use Google Scholar in bibliometrics? Broken out by Annual Tuition Level

Annual Tuition Level	Yes	No
less than $9000	54,55%	45,45%
$9000 - $14000	90,00%	10,00%
more than $14000	100,00%	0,00%

Table 5.4.5 Does your library use Google Scholar in bibliometrics? Broken out by FTE Student Enrollment

FTE Student Enrollment	Yes	No
less than 11000	81,82%	18,18%
11000 - 22000	90,00%	10,00%
more than 22000	70,00%	30,00%

Table 5.4.6 Does your library use Google Scholar in bibliometrics? Broken out by Carnegie Class

Carnegie Class	Yes	No
4-Year College	75,00%	25,00%
MA/PHD Granting	77,78%	22,22%
Research University	83,33%	16,67%

Table 5.5.1 Does your library use Journal Citation Reports citation indices in bibliometrics?

	No Answer	Yes	No
Entire sample	0,00%	77,42%	22,58%

Table 5.5.2 Does your library use Journal Citation Reports citation indices in bibliometrics? Broken out by Country

Country	Yes	No
USA	58,33%	41,67%
UK / Ireland	90,00%	10,00%
All Other	88,89%	11,11%

Table 5.5.3 Does your library use Journal Citation Reports citation indices in bibliometrics? Broken out by Type of College

Type of College	Yes	No
Public	77,78%	22,22%
Private	75,00%	25,00%

Table 5.5.4 Does your library use Journal Citation Reports citation indices in bibliometrics? Broken out by Annual Tuition Level

Annual Tuition Level	Yes	No
less than $9000	72,73%	27,27%
$9000 - $14000	80,00%	20,00%
more than $14000	80,00%	20,00%

Table 5.5.5 Does your library use Journal Citation Reports citation indices in bibliometrics? Broken out by FTE Student Enrollment

FTE Student Enrollment	Yes	No
less than 11000	81,82%	18,18%
11000 - 22000	70,00%	30,00%
more than 22000	80,00%	20,00%

Table 5.5.6 Does your library use Journal Citation Reports citation indices in bibliometrics? Broken out by Carnegie Class

Carnegie Class	Yes	No
4-Year College	50,00%	50,00%
MA/PHD Granting	88,89%	11,11%
Research University	77,78%	22,22%

Does your library use other citation indices in bibliometrics?

1) Incites; Publish or Perish, Scimago J&CR, Leiden,
2) Publish or Perish
3) altmetrics.com
4) Essential Science Indicators (also from Thomson Reuters)
5) InCites, Publish or Perish

Discuss your experience with Google Scholar as a citation analysis tool.

1) Used only when the Thomson Reuters or Scopus metrics do not cover the subject area or if an overview of grey literature citations are needed.
2) Somewhat better coverage than Web of Science.
3) I have used it to find who cites a work.
4) It is confused and confusing. much duplication
5) Ubiquitous but not rigorous enough to be relied upon.
6) unreliable for bibliometrics analyses (many duplicates), but useful for literature search
7) Very easy to create author/researcher profiles; citation counts usually higher than those in Web of Science or Scopus; checks I have done indicate that Google Scholar citations are fairly accurate, given that Scopus and Web of Science also have errors.
8) I personally use the My Citations feature of Google Scholar and at least show it to others. I have used Harzing's Publish or Perish (which incorporates Google Scholar data).
9) run citation analysis report regularly for individuals and departments. Also advise on using Google Scholar Citations
10) Wary as vastly higher numbers than WoS/Scopus. Suspect lack of quality control / phantom citations
11) Its ok
12) Poor data quality
13) PoP software is good. Data extraction limitations of GS are hampering any real bibliometrics research
14) Google Scholar is good for creating individual profile with citation information and can be used with Publish or Perish software to do some analyses but in general Google Scholar is very limited as a citation analysis tool.
15) we show it to Researchers, but don't use it ourselves
16) Not used much except by individual faculty
17) Hit and miss - many duplicates, but also identifies unique citations. Not viewed as credible by funding agencies though.
18) I do not used as such, but I use Publish or Perish which is based on GS data. The results from PoP are usually acceptable.
19) Useful but a bit flaky due to occasional bad metadata
20) It's been helpful for non-STEM faculty, but attitudes differ around campus. Some think it overinflates citations, while others see it as the only accurate tool to measure citations in their field.
21) It is a useful tool with inconsistency
22) h-index
23) n/a
24) Problems with GS data and inflated citation counts. Use the Publish or Perish software to try and remedy this.
25) I often use the cited by feature in Google Scholar to find articles that are relevant

26) It is nice but alone does not capture the full story as it is not very up to date

27) Covers a wide collection of mentions, citations etc. but generally comes up with similar citation figures to other resources

28) Use it in combination with other tools to help identify and collate citation metrics for individual faculty members. Caution is used and taught

Table 6.1 How heavily used is the SciMago Journal Ranking system at your institution?

	No Answer	Unaware of it	Not Used Much	Used Somewhat	Used a Lot	Used a Great Deal
Entire sample	3,23%	25,81%	29,03%	38,71%	3,23%	0,00%

Table 6.2 How heavily used is the SciMago Journal Ranking system at your institution? Broken out by Country

Country	No Answer	Unaware of it	Not Used Much	Used Somewhat	Used a Lot	Used a Great Deal
USA	8,33%	50,00%	16,67%	25,00%	0,00%	0,00%
UK / Ireland	0,00%	20,00%	40,00%	40,00%	0,00%	0,00%
All Other	0,00%	0,00%	33,33%	55,56%	11,11%	0,00%

Table 6.3 How heavily used is the SciMago Journal Ranking system at your institution? Broken out by Type of College

Type of College	No Answer	Unaware of it	Not Used Much	Used Somewhat	Used a Lot	Used a Great Deal
Public	3,70%	22,22%	29,63%	40,74%	3,70%	0,00%
Private	0,00%	50,00%	25,00%	25,00%	0,00%	0,00%

Table 6.4 How heavily used is the SciMago Journal Ranking system at your institution? Broken out by Annual Tuition Level

Annual Tuition Level	No Answer	Unaware of it	Not Used Much	Used Somewhat	Used a Lot	Used a Great Deal
less than $9000	9,09%	18,18%	36,36%	27,27%	9,09%	0,00%
$9000 - $14000	0,00%	30,00%	30,00%	40,00%	0,00%	0,00%
more than $14000	0,00%	30,00%	20,00%	50,00%	0,00%	0,00%

Table 6.5 How heavily used is the SciMago Journal Ranking system at your institution? Broken out by FTE Student Enrollment

FTE Student Enrollment	No Answer	Unaware of it	Not Used Much	Used Somewhat	Used a Lot	Used a Great Deal
less than 11000	0,00%	27,27%	36,36%	36,36%	0,00%	0,00%
11000 - 22000	0,00%	30,00%	20,00%	50,00%	0,00%	0,00%
more than 22000	10,00%	20,00%	30,00%	30,00%	10,00%	0,00%

Table 6.6 How heavily used is the SciMago Journal Ranking system at your institution? Broken out by Carnegie Class

Carnegie Class	No Answer	Unaware of it	Not Used Much	Used Somewhat	Used a Lot	Used a Great Deal
4-Year College	0,00%	50,00%	25,00%	0,00%	25,00%	0,00%
MA/PHD Granting	0,00%	11,11%	33,33%	55,56%	0,00%	0,00%
Research University	5,56%	27,78%	27,78%	38,89%	0,00%	0,00%

Table 7.1 Over the Past three years, how has funding for bibliometrics research, staff and services at your library changed?

	No Answer	Diminished Significantly	Diminished	Remained Approximately the Same	Increased	Increased Significantly
Entire sample	6,45%	3,23%	9,68%	45,16%	25,81%	9,68%

Table 7.2 Over the Past three years, how has funding for bibliometrics research, staff and services at your library changed? Broken out by Country

Country	No Answer	Diminished Significantly	Diminished	Remained Approximately the Same	Increased	Increased Significantly
USA	8,33%	8,33%	8,33%	66,67%	8,33%	0,00%
UK / Ireland	0,00%	0,00%	10,00%	40,00%	40,00%	10,00%
All Other	11,11%	0,00%	11,11%	22,22%	33,33%	22,22%

Table 7.3 Over the Past three years, how has funding for bibliometrics research, staff and services at your library changed? Broken out by Type of College

Type of College	No Answer	Diminished Significantly	Diminished	Remained Approximately the Same	Increased	Increased Significantly
Public	7,41%	0,00%	11,11%	44,44%	25,93%	11,11%
Private	0,00%	25,00%	0,00%	50,00%	25,00%	0,00%

Table 7.4 Over the Past three years, how has funding for bibliometrics research, staff and services at your library changed? Broken out by Annual Tuition Level

Annual Tuition Level	No Answer	Diminished Significantly	Diminished	Remained Approximately the Same	Increased	Increased Significantly
less than $9000	18,18%	0,00%	27,27%	9,09%	27,27%	18,18%
$9000 - $14000	0,00%	10,00%	0,00%	70,00%	10,00%	10,00%
more than $14000	0,00%	0,00%	0,00%	60,00%	40,00%	0,00%

Table 7.5 Over the Past three years, how has funding for bibliometrics research, staff and services at your library changed? Broken out by FTE Student Enrollment

FTE Student Enrollment	No Answer	Diminished Significantly	Diminished	Remained Approximately the Same	Increased	Increased Significantly
less than 11000	0,00%	9,09%	18,18%	18,18%	36,36%	18,18%
11000 - 22000	10,00%	0,00%	0,00%	80,00%	10,00%	0,00%
more than 22000	10,00%	0,00%	10,00%	40,00%	30,00%	10,00%

Table 7.6 Over the Past three years, how has funding for bibliometrics research, staff and services at your library changed?: Broken out by Carnegie Class

Carnegie Class	No Answer	Diminished Significantly	Diminished	Remained Approximately the Same	Increased	Increased Significantly
4-Year College	0,00%	0,00%	25,00%	50,00%	25,00%	0,00%
MA/PHD Granting	11,11%	0,00%	11,11%	55,56%	11,11%	11,11%
Research University	5,56%	5,56%	5,56%	38,89%	33,33%	11,11%

Table 8.1 Which phrase best describes how your library staffs its bibliometrics services?

	No Answer	We have a dedicated staff of bibliometrics specialists	We have on. E real specialist and others who work part time on the issue	It is one specialty among others for a number of librarians but no specific staff or position	Honestly we do not have too much expertize in this area
Entire sample	3,23%	6,45%	22,58%	54,84%	12,90%

Table 8.2 Which phrase best describes how your library staffs its bibliometrics services? Broken out by Country

Country	No Answer	We have a dedicated staff of bibliometrics specialists	We have on real specialist and others who work part time on the issue	It is one specialty among others for a number of librarians but no specific staff or position	Honestly we do not have too much expertize in this area
USA	8,33%	0,00%	8,33%	66,67%	16,67%
UK / Ireland	0,00%	0,00%	40,00%	60,00%	0,00%
All Other	0,00%	22,22%	22,22%	33,33%	22,22%

Table 8.3 Which phrase best describes how your library staffs its bibliometrics services? Broken out by Type of College

Type of College	No Answer	We have a dedicated staff of bibliometrics specialists	We have on real specialist and others who work part time on the issue	It is one specialty among others for a number of librarians but no specific staff or position	Honestly we do not have too much expertize in this area
Public	3,70%	7,41%	22,22%	55,56%	11,11%
Private	0,00%	0,00%	25,00%	50,00%	25,00%

Table 8.4 Which phrase best describes how your library staffs its bibliometrics services? Broken out by Annual Tuition Level

Annual Tuition Level	No Answer	We have a dedicated staff of bibliometrics specialists	We have on real specialist and others who work part time on the issue	It is one specialty among others for a number of librarians but no specific staff or position	Honestly we do not have too much expertize in this area
less than $9000	9,09%	18,18%	18,18%	27,27%	27,27%
$9000 - $14000	0,00%	0,00%	30,00%	70,00%	0,00%
more than $14000	0,00%	0,00%	20,00%	70,00%	10,00%

Table 8.5 Which phrase best describes how your library staffs its bibliometrics services? Broken out by FTE Student Enrollment

FTE Student Enrollment	No Answer	We have a dedicated staff of bibliometrics specialists	We have on real specialist and others who work part time on the issue	It is one specialty among others for a number of librarians but no specific staff or position	Honestly we do not have too much expertize in this area
less than 11000	0,00%	9,09%	45,45%	27,27%	18,18%
11000 - 22000	0,00%	0,00%	0,00%	80,00%	20,00%
more than 22000	10,00%	10,00%	20,00%	60,00%	0,00%

Table 8.6 Which phrase best describes how your library staffs its bibliometrics services? Broken out by Carnegie Class

Carnegie Class	No Answer	We have a dedicated staff of bibliometrics specialists	We have on real specialist and others who work part time on the issue	It is one specialty among others for a number of librarians but no specific staff or position	Honestly we do not have too much expertize in this area
4-Year College	0,00%	0,00%	0,00%	100,00%	0,00%
MA/PHD Granting	0,00%	11,11%	0,00%	55,56%	33,33%
Research University	5,56%	5,56%	38,89%	44,44%	5,56%

Table 9.1 What is the outlook for funding at your library for bibliometrics staff and services over the next few years?

	No Answer	Likely to Diminish Significantly	Likely to Diminish	Likely to Remain Approximately the Same	Likely to Increase	Likely to Increase Significantly
Entire sample	3,23%	3,23%	6,45%	51,61%	35,48%	0,00%

Table 9.2 What is the outlook for funding at your library for bibliometrics staff and services over the next few years? Broken out by Country

Country	No Answer	Likely to Diminish Significantly	Likely to Diminish	Likely to Remain Approximately the Same	Likely to Increase	Likely to Increase Significantly
USA	8,33%	8,33%	16,67%	50,00%	16,67%	0,00%
UK / Ireland	0,00%	0,00%	0,00%	60,00%	40,00%	0,00%
All Other	0,00%	0,00%	0,00%	44,44%	55,56%	0,00%

Table 9.3 What is the outlook for funding at your library for bibliometrics staff and services over the next few years? Broken out by Type of College

Type of College	No Answer	Likely to Diminish Significantly	Likely to Diminish	Likely to Remain Approximately the Same	Likely to Increase	Likely to Increase Significantly
Public	3,70%	3,70%	3,70%	51,85%	37,04%	0,00%
Private	0,00%	0,00%	25,00%	50,00%	25,00%	0,00%

Table 9.4 What is the outlook for funding at your library for bibliometrics staff and services over the next few years? Broken out by Annual Tuition Level

Annual Tuition Level	No Answer	Likely to Diminish Significantly	Likely to Diminish	Likely to Remain Approximately the Same	Likely to Increase	Likely to Increase Significantly
less than $9000	9,09%	0,00%	9,09%	27,27%	54,55%	0,00%
$9000 - $14000	0,00%	10,00%	10,00%	60,00%	20,00%	0,00%
more than $14000	0,00%	0,00%	0,00%	70,00%	30,00%	0,00%

Table 9.5 What is the outlook for funding at your library for bibliometrics staff and services over the next few years? Broken out by FTE Student Enrollment

FTE Student Enrollment	No Answer	Likely to Diminish Significantly	Likely to Diminish	Likely to Remain Approximately the Same	Likely to Increase	Likely to Increase Significantly
less than 11000	0,00%	0,00%	18,18%	54,55%	27,27%	0,00%
11000 - 22000	0,00%	0,00%	0,00%	60,00%	40,00%	0,00%
more than 22000	10,00%	10,00%	0,00%	40,00%	40,00%	0,00%

Table 9.6 What is the outlook for Funding at your library for bibliometrics staff and services over the next few years? Broken out by Carnegie Class

Carnegie Class	No Answer	Likely to Diminish Significantly	Likely to Diminish	Likely to Remain Approximately the Same	Likely to Increase	Likely to Increase Significantly
4-Year College	0,00%	0,00%	0,00%	50,00%	50,00%	0,00%
MA/PHD Granting	0,00%	0,00%	0,00%	77,78%	22,22%	0,00%
Research University	5,56%	5,56%	11,11%	38,89%	38,89%	0,00%

Table 10.1 What do you think of the bibliometrics capabilities of your own library or department of library science?

	Excellent	Good	Acceptable	Poor
Entire sample	6,45%	25,81%	51,61%	16,13%

Table 10.2 What do you think of the bibliometrics capabilities of your own library or department of library science? Broken out by Country

Country	Excellent	Good	Acceptable	Poor
USA	8,33%	16,67%	50,00%	25,00%
UK / Ireland	0,00%	40,00%	60,00%	0,00%
All Other	11,11%	22,22%	44,44%	22,22%

Table 10.3 What do you think of the bibliometrics capabilities of your own library or department of library science? Broken out by Type of College

Type of College	Excellent	Good	Acceptable	Poor
Public	3,70%	29,63%	51,85%	14,81%
Private	25,00%	0,00%	50,00%	25,00%

Table 10.4 What do you think of the bibliometrics capabilities of your own library or department of library science? Broken out by Annual Tuition Level

Annual Tuition Level	Excellent	Good	Acceptable	Poor
less than $9000	9,09%	18,18%	45,45%	27,27%
$9000 - $14000	0,00%	30,00%	70,00%	0,00%
more than $14000	10,00%	30,00%	40,00%	20,00%

Table 10.5 What do you think of the bibliometrics capabilities of your own library or department of library science? Broken out by FTE Student Enrollment

FTE Student Enrollment	Excellent	Good	Acceptable	Poor
less than 11000	9,09%	36,36%	36,36%	18,18%
11000 - 22000	10,00%	20,00%	60,00%	10,00%
more than 22000	0,00%	20,00%	60,00%	20,00%

Table 10.6 What do you think of the bibliometrics capabilities of your own library or department of library science? Broken out by Carnegie Class

Carnegie Class	Excellent	Good	Acceptable	Poor
4-Year College	0,00%	0,00%	75,00%	25,00%
MA/PHD Granting	11,11%	22,22%	44,44%	22,22%
Research University	5,56%	33,33%	50,00%	11,11%

Table 11.1 Demand for bibliometrics services at your library in the past two years has:

	No Answer	Fallen considerably	Fallen somewhat	Remained about the same	Increased somewhat	Increased considerably
Entire sample	3,23%	0,00%	0,00%	25,81%	48,39%	22,58%

Table 11.2 Demand for bibliometrics services at your library in the past two years has: Broken out by Country

Country	No Answer	Fallen considerably	Fallen somewhat	Remained about the same	Increased somewhat	Increased considerably
USA	8,33%	0,00%	0,00%	50,00%	41,67%	0,00%
UK / Ireland	0,00%	0,00%	0,00%	0,00%	60,00%	40,00%
All Other	0,00%	0,00%	0,00%	22,22%	44,44%	33,33%

Table 11.3 Demand for bibliometrics services at your library in the past two years has: Broken out by Type of College

Type of College	No Answer	Fallen considerably	Fallen somewhat	Remained about the same	Increased somewhat	Increased considerably
Public	3,70%	0,00%	0,00%	22,22%	48,15%	25,93%
Private	0,00%	0,00%	0,00%	50,00%	50,00%	0,00%

Table 11.4 Demand for bibliometrics services at your library in the past two years has: Broken out by Annual Tuition Level

Annual Tuition Level	No Answer	Fallen considerably	Fallen somewhat	Remained about the same	Increased somewhat	Increased considerably
less than $9000	9,09%	0,00%	0,00%	27,27%	45,45%	18,18%
$9000 - $14000	0,00%	0,00%	0,00%	20,00%	50,00%	30,00%
more than $14000	0,00%	0,00%	0,00%	30,00%	50,00%	20,00%

Table 11.5 Demand for bibliometrics services at your library in the past two years has: Broken out by FTE Student Enrollment

FTE Student Enrollment	No Answer	Fallen considerably	Fallen somewhat	Remained about the same	Increased somewhat	Increased considerably
less than 11000	0,00%	0,00%	0,00%	18,18%	45,45%	36,36%
11000 - 22000	0,00%	0,00%	0,00%	40,00%	60,00%	0,00%
more than 22000	10,00%	0,00%	0,00%	20,00%	40,00%	30,00%

Table 11.6 Demand for bibliometrics services at your library in the past two years has: Broken out by Carnegie Class

Carnegie Class	No Answer	Fallen considerably	Fallen somewhat	Remained about the same	Increased somewhat	Increased considerably
4-Year College	0,00%	0,00%	0,00%	50,00%	50,00%	0,00%
MA/PHD Granting	0,00%	0,00%	0,00%	55,56%	33,33%	11,11%
Research University	5,56%	0,00%	0,00%	5,56%	55,56%	33,33%

Which academic or administrative departments request the most assistance for bibliometrics services?

1) Our director's office for use in strategic decisions
2) Science, Education and Language Studies, Educational Technology
3) Individual faculty sometimes request assistance with bibliometrics for tenure and promotion; other colleges may have higher demand and service level for this type of request. College administrators are becoming interested in better bibliometrics for faculty reporting.
4) administrative person in charge of assessment
5) We are only biomedical research. All of them. 75 laboratory based "departments"
6) Research Office, Planning.
7) Board of Directors
8) Individual researchers for promotion and other applications
9) We don't really offer it formally yet, but I'm charged with kicking it off. Computer Science has come to me personally for help.
10) research managers, heads of departments
11) Engineering and Science.
12) Research office and external peer reviews
13) Computer science Sociology
14) All
15) Faculty of Management
16) Medicine and health, some science disciplines and engineering
17) engineering arts and sciences
18) STEM departments
19) Life Sciences
20) academic departments in general
21) sciences and engineering
22) this is strictly done within the library for collection assessment purposes
23) All researchers seeking a rating from the National Research Foundation
24) Ministry
25) Science depts.
26) Institutional Analysis & Planning, Office of Research, individual faculty members, research groups

As a general average, how would you rate the skill of your college's faculty in developing, understanding and using bibliometrics evaluations?

1) Above average
2) is increasing awareness in some areas
3) varied
4) good
5) very low
6) Potential - excellent; Current state - average.
7) Advanced
8) Low in the humanities and social sciences, moderate in the life and physical sciences but both areas of research cover the full spectrum from little understanding to expert understanding.
9) Catch as catch can. Overall - Poor.
10) aware of the tools but very little experience in using them
11) Fairly limited
12) Very good
13) Fair
14) Love the reports we provide them with
15) Average to poor
16) OK
17) Poor
18) Average
19) Fair
20) average, but well below average with altmetrics
21) A few are good, many are not
22) Average - most are only aware of JCR/Web of Science and/or Google Scholar.
23) low skill
24) adequate but not necessarily current with new metrics
25) n/a
26) We have been growing awareness, but they rely on the library and the institutions research office for these services
27) OK
28) Gaining understanding over time
29) As a whole the Library is just beginning to develop, understand, and use bibliometrics at a variety of levels within the University. Individual librarians have assisted individual faculty members with bibliometrics activities related to Tenure & promotion and grant applications.

Table 12.1 Have you or those working with you in your bibliometrics services ever felt pressure to alter methodologies to produce evaluations or results that may lead to more favorable evaluations of a colleges, department or individual faculty member's scholarly output?

	No Answer	Yes	No
Entire sample	3,23%	6,45%	90,32%

Table 12.2 Have you or those working with you in your bibliometrics services ever felt pressure to alter methodologies to produce evaluations or results that may lead to more favorable evaluations of a colleges, department or individual faculty member's scholarly output? Broken out by Country

Country	No Answer	Yes	No
USA	8,33%	8,33%	83,33%
UK / Ireland	0,00%	0,00%	100,00%
All Other	0,00%	11,11%	88,89%

Table 12.3 Have you or those working with you in your bibliometrics services ever felt pressure to alter methodologies to produce evaluations or results that may lead to more favorable evaluations of a colleges, department or individual faculty member's scholarly output? Broken out by Type of College

Type of College	No Answer	Yes	No
Public	3,70%	3,70%	92,59%
Private	0,00%	25,00%	75,00%

Table 12.4 Have you or those working with you in your bibliometrics services ever felt pressure to alter methodologies to produce evaluations or results that may lead to more favorable evaluations of a colleges, department or individual faculty member's scholarly output? Broken out by Annual Tuition Level

Annual Tuition Level	No Answer	Yes	No
less than $9000	9,09%	9,09%	81,82%
$9000 - $14000	0,00%	10,00%	90,00%
more than $14000	0,00%	0,00%	100,00%

Table 12.5 Have you or those working with you in your bibliometrics services ever felt pressure to alter methodologies to produce evaluations or results that may lead to more favorable evaluations of a colleges, department or individual faculty member's scholarly output? Broken out by FTE Student Enrollment

FTE Student Enrollment	No Answer	Yes	No
less than 11000	0,00%	18,18%	81,82%
11000 - 22000	0,00%	0,00%	100,00%
more than 22000	10,00%	0,00%	90,00%

Table 12.6 Have you or those working with you in your bibliometrics services ever felt pressure to alter methodologies to produce evaluations or results that may lead to more favorable evaluations of a colleges, department or individual faculty member's scholarly output? Broken out by Carnegie Class

Carnegie Class	No Answer	Yes	No
4-Year College	0,00%	0,00%	100,00%
MA/PHD Granting	0,00%	11,11%	88,89%
Research University	5,56%	5,56%	88,89%

Table 13.1 To the best of your knowledge do any departments of your college require some form of bibliometrics analysis be done in tenure decision making or hiring decisions?

	No Answer	Yes	No	Do not really know
Entire sample	3,23%	51,61%	22,58%	22,58%

Table 13.2 To the best of your knowledge do any departments of your college require some form of bibliometrics analysis be done in tenure decision making or hiring decisions? Broken out by Country

Country	No Answer	Yes	No	Do not really know
USA	8,33%	50,00%	25,00%	16,67%
UK / Ireland	0,00%	30,00%	30,00%	40,00%
All Other	0,00%	77,78%	11,11%	11,11%

Table 13.3 To the best of your knowledge do any departments of your college require some form of bibliometrics analysis be done in tenure decision making or hiring decisions? Broken out by Type of College

Type of College	No Answer	Yes	No	Do not really know
Public	3,70%	55,56%	18,52%	22,22%
Private	0,00%	25,00%	50,00%	25,00%

Table 13.4 To the best of your knowledge do any departments of your college require some form of bibliometrics analysis be done in tenure decision making or hiring decisions? Broken out by Annual Tuition Level

Annual Tuition Level	No Answer	Yes	No	Do not really know
less than $9000	9,09%	54,55%	27,27%	9,09%
$9000 - $14000	0,00%	50,00%	30,00%	20,00%
more than $14000	0,00%	50,00%	10,00%	40,00%

Table 13.5 To the best of your knowledge do any departments of your college require some form of bibliometrics analysis be done in tenure decision making or hiring decisions? Broken out by FTE Student Enrollment

FTE Student Enrollment	No Answer	Yes	No	Do not really know
less than 11000	0,00%	36,36%	45,45%	18,18%
11000 - 22000	0,00%	60,00%	0,00%	40,00%
more than 22000	10,00%	60,00%	20,00%	10,00%

Table 13.6 To the best of your knowledge do any departments of your college require some form of bibliometrics analysis be done in tenure decision making or hiring decisions? Broken out by Carnegie Class

Carnegie Class	No Answer	Yes	No	Do not really know
4-Year College	0,00%	25,00%	50,00%	25,00%
MA/PHD Granting	0,00%	55,56%	11,11%	33,33%
Research University	5,56%	55,56%	22,22%	16,67%

Describe what role if any the academic library plays in providing bibliometrics services during the tenure review process at different departments of your institution.

1) None
2) None
3) None
4) Johnson Graduate School of Management (I think, not positive) - librarians provide a high level of service.
5) None that I know of
6) Doesn't in tenure decisions. Is used more to impress and inform Board of Trustees of the success and influence of our science.
7) None
8) Provide a list of publications along with basic bibliometrics indicators
9) Assist researchers to create, update and maintain their online profiles in ResearcherID, Scopus and Google Scholar. These sources are then used for identifying citation profiles. Publish or Perish (http://www.harzing.com/pop.htm) is another tool that we used to use, but rarely use now.
10) None yet ... I don't know what will be in store.
11) provide metrics data
12) I believe different departments/libraries help out.
13) No role
14) It is only for the newly tenured professors that the library will execute a full bibliometrics analysis of the potential candidates
15) The Library currently has no role
16) we will provide analysis of applying researchers
17) Librarians might be asked for advice
18) Assist with profile building in Symplectic and ensuring all records where possible are linking to Scopus/WoS records to ensure H-Index and citation counts are reliable. Assistance with generating graphs.
19) Occasionally we have a request for a specific case.
20) We provide instruction of tools and understanding the concepts of bibliometrics, including altmetrics
21) Not applicable in the UK
22) We have a LibGuide, have provided workshops in the past, and offer one-on-one assistance.
23) only for consultation and assistance
24) general overview
25) we fund JCR
26) Searches on Web of Science to provide the H-index of researchers and use of Google Scholar profiles
27) We do not have tenure
28) N/A
29) Library not involved as far as I know

Describe the library's role, if any, in advising your institution's office of research grants, technology licensing or other divisions about their use of bibliometrics and other tools in measuring the impact of scholarly output.

1) None
2) None
3) Minimal
4) Very little, may grow with VIVO and other tools.
5) We have not done that.
6) None
7) Have regular meetings with Schools, Planning, and RO about this. We are the only provider of institutional training and support in this area.
8) Provide a wide variety of bibliometrics analysis
9) Advise about new tools and other new information on a casual basis as we continue to build a working relationship.
10) A number of years ago I provided guidance to the Vice-Provost for Research. I brought to the surface the cautions that need to go along with the data.
11) Unknown
12) Early stages
13) Point of contact. Advise where possible.
14) No role
15) Used a lot in assisting staff to quantify their standing in their field.
16) The Research Office has their own bibliometrics expert but I would discuss things with her but it isn't a very formal advising role.
17) we will see
18) None
19) Research Office and Library work jointly on many research output projects and co-fund the purchase of research analysis tools such as Incites.
20) No we do not do that.
21) our role is limited but is something we're striving towards
22) We get occasional requests
23) We have no role, though we would love to be included in the conversation.
24) No role
25) sparse, but hoping to increase
26) n/a
27) The library does not advise but does work together with them when they require information
28) None
29) Occasional guidance provided when requested. Some expertise already exists in the Research Office

Table 14.1 Does the library play any role in tracking collaboration networks of scholars in different subjects and countries to measure trends in collaboration between countries, institutions or even academic disciplines?

	No Answer	Yes	No
Entire sample	6,45%	32,26%	61,29%

Table 14.2 Does the library play any role in tracking collaboration networks of scholars in different subjects and countries to measure trends in collaboration between countries, institutions or even academic disciplines? Broken out by Country

Country	No Answer	Yes	No
USA	0,00%	25,00%	75,00%
UK / Ireland	10,00%	30,00%	60,00%
All Other	11,11%	44,44%	44,44%

Table 14.3 Does the library play any role in tracking collaboration networks of scholars in different subjects and countries to measure trends in collaboration between countries, institutions or even academic disciplines? Broken out by Type of College

Type of College	No Answer	Yes	No
Public	7,41%	33,33%	59,26%
Private	0,00%	25,00%	75,00%

Table 14.4 Does the library play any role in tracking collaboration networks of scholars in different subjects and countries to measure trends in collaboration between countries, institutions or even academic disciplines? Broken out by Annual Tuition Level

Annual Tuition Level	No Answer	Yes	No
less than $9000	9,09%	27,27%	63,64%
$9000 - $14000	0,00%	40,00%	60,00%
more than $14000	10,00%	30,00%	60,00%

Table 14.5 Does the library play any role in tracking collaboration networks of scholars in different subjects and countries to measure trends in collaboration between countries, institutions or even academic disciplines? Broken out by FTE Student Enrollment

FTE Student Enrollment	No Answer	Yes	No
less than 11000	0,00%	45,45%	54,55%
11000 - 22000	10,00%	20,00%	70,00%
more than 22000	10,00%	30,00%	60,00%

Table 14.6 Does the library play any role in tracking collaboration networks of scholars in different subjects and countries to measure trends in collaboration between countries, institutions or even academic disciplines? Broken out by Carnegie Class

Carnegie Class	No Answer	Yes	No
4-Year College	0,00%	0,00%	100,00%
MA/PHD Granting	0,00%	22,22%	77,78%
Research University	11,11%	44,44%	44,44%

If the library plays any role in tracking collaboration networks of scholars in different subjects and countries to measure trends in collaboration between countries, institutions or even academic disciplines, what is that role?

1) We collaborate extensively with other institutions, particularly in the developing world and we use bibliometrics to track collaborations with key institutions and to track the top performing institutions within specific subject areas.
2) Implementing VIVO gives us this capability; we know anecdotally that some deans use it for this purpose.
3) Any such analysis is done by us. usually for a Board meeting
4) Out of curiosity, to try and promote interest in bibliometrics as a tool.
5) Provide a wide variety of bibliometrics analysis
6) Research office role with support from the library
7) Indicate what collaboration has taken place, the impact of the papers from that collaboration.
8) not 100% clear yet
9) Assistance with generating reports
10) Responding to request for colleges or departments which happen occasionally.
11) This is one of our librarian's research interests but we as a library don't track this.
12) We are beginning to look at it from the stand point of interdisciplinarity and international partnerships
13) Have done international collaboration analyses in the past

What efforts has your library made in providing alternatives to traditional biometric techniques, alternatives which are often described under the banner "altmetrics"?

1) None
2) Altmetrics are displayed on our institutional repository
3) Have altmetrics on our institutional repository
4) Basic online library guides, informal discussion with faculty
5) I am not aware of the use of alternative metrics at our library
6) Have tried to communicate to Administrative groups (office of the President) that multi-dimensional analyses would be a more complete picture. Doesn't always work.
7) I think the term you are looking for is "alt-metrics" and yes we draw attention to them in our training sessions.
8) Huhu. Please be advised that neither "biometric" nor "altimetrics" are correct (NOTED) terms. We use some like network analysis
9) We promote and explain altmetrics as a concept, we display the altmetrics.com donuts in researcher portfolio profiles and will soon display these donuts in repository records. We have an altmetrics page in a Measuring Research Impact LibGuide.
10) We are exploring tools now, but nothing is in place yet.
11) altmetric donut embedded into Institutional Repository
12) Early days - embedded in CRIS / repository. Doing some work on ranking
13) Some departments/libraries have.
14) Little
15) We are working better reporting our own download statistics and will look in the coming years at a possible tool such as Plum, impactstory or altmetrics.com. If not on the basis of PLoS api etc.
16) The Library has promoted and given information on altmetrics in workshops.
17) we Show that to scholars and teach the directors board
18) None
19) Altmetrics included in our research performance system (Symplectic). Library is also going to trial Almetrics.Explorer and Plum Analytics
20) Only when requested; and as a complement to traditional methods
21) we're working towards including PlumX with our repository (which will be up and running early 2015), and we have two designated research librarians to encourage open science and leveraging it with altmetrics
22) We run a research workshop on the topic. Isn't it altmetrics?
23) It's covered in our research guide and mentioned in workshops.
24) Only training
25) Sparse
26) Developing awareness of altmetrics through during information literacy training and presentations at symposiums
27) None

28) Still at the level of sensitizing faculty and the university community at large
29) Some awareness raising and blogging

Table 15.1 How much confidence do you have that altmetric methods have already or will become reliable and competitive means of evaluating scholarly output similar to traditional bibliometrics methods?

	No Answer	They are superior to and will eventually supplant traditional methods	They are already important and competitive with traditional methods	They are an adjunct and useful but subordinate methodology	They are more or less a fad and don't really add much	They are misleading and more or less a waste of time
Entire sample	3,23%	0,00%	32,26%	61,29%	3,23%	0,00%

Table 15.2 How much confidence do you have that altmetric methods have already or will become reliable and competitive means of evaluating scholarly output similar to traditional bibliometrics methods? Broken out by Country

Country	No Answer	They are superior to and will eventually supplant traditional methods	They are already important and competitive with traditional methods	They are an adjunct and useful but subordinate methodology	They are more or less a fad and don't really add much	They are misleading and more or less a waste of time
USA	0,00%	0,00%	33,33%	58,33%	8,33%	0,00%
UK / Ireland	0,00%	0,00%	40,00%	60,00%	0,00%	0,00%
All Other	11,11%	0,00%	22,22%	66,67%	0,00%	0,00%

Table 15.3 How much confidence do you have that altmetric methods have already or will become reliable and competitive means of evaluating scholarly output similar to traditional bibliometrics methods? Broken out by Type of College

Type of College	No Answer	They are superior to and will eventually supplant traditional methods	They are already important and competitive with traditional methods	They are an adjunct and useful but subordinate methodology	They are more or less a fad and don't really add much	They are misleading and more or less a waste of time
Public	3,70%	0,00%	37,04%	55,56%	3,70%	0,00%
Private	0,00%	0,00%	0,00%	100,00%	0,00%	0,00%

Table 15.4 How much confidence do you have that altmetric methods have already or will become reliable and competitive means of evaluating scholarly output similar to traditional bibliometrics methods? Broken out by Annual Tuition Level

Annual Tuition Level	No Answer	They are superior to and will eventually supplant traditional methods	They are already important and competitive with traditional methods	They are an adjunct and useful but subordinate methodology	They are more or less a fad and don't really add much	They are misleading and more or less a waste of time
less than $9000	9,09%	0,00%	18,18%	63,64%	9,09%	0,00%
$9000 - $14000	0,00%	0,00%	50,00%	50,00%	0,00%	0,00%
more than $14000	0,00%	0,00%	30,00%	70,00%	0,00%	0,00%

Table 15.5 How much confidence do you have that altmetric methods have already or will become reliable and competitive means of evaluating scholarly output similar to traditional bibliometrics methods? Broken out by FTE Student Enrollment

FTE Student Enrollment	No Answer	They are superior to and will eventually supplant traditional methods	They are already important and competitive with traditional methods	They are an adjunct and useful but subordinate methodology	They are more or less a fad and don't really add much	They are misleading and more or less a waste of time
less than 11000	0,00%	0,00%	27,27%	72,73%	0,00%	0,00%
11000 - 22000	0,00%	0,00%	30,00%	70,00%	0,00%	0,00%
more than 22000	10,00%	0,00%	40,00%	40,00%	10,00%	0,00%

Table 15.6 How much confidence do you have that altmetric methods have already or will become reliable and competitive means of evaluating scholarly output similar to traditional bibliometrics methods? Broken out by Carnegie Class

Carnegie Class	No Answer	They are superior to and will eventually supplant traditional methods	They are already important and competitive with traditional methods	They are an adjunct and useful but subordinate methodology	They are more or less a fad and don't really add much	They are misleading and more or less a waste of time
4-Year College	0,00%	0,00%	50,00%	50,00%	0,00%	0,00%
MA/PHD Granting	0,00%	0,00%	22,22%	77,78%	0,00%	0,00%
Research University	5,56%	0,00%	33,33%	55,56%	5,56%	0,00%

Table 16.1 How much annual staff time in hours would you say that your library staff expends in teaching faculty about publication lists and rankings, citation impact tools and methods, and other bibliometrics and citation analysis processes and procedures? (one person working full time would be about 1850 hours)

	Mean	Median	Minimum	Maximum
Entire sample	346,27	90,00	0,00	1850,00

Table 16.2 How much annual staff time in hours would you say that your library staff expends in teaching faculty about publication lists and rankings, citation impact tools and methods, and other bibliometrics and citation analysis processes and procedures? (One person working full time would be about 1850 hours) Broken out by Country

Country	Mean	Median	Minimum	Maximum
USA	160,30	37,50	0,00	693,00
UK / Ireland	539,44	50,00	15,00	1850,00
All Other	363,57	100,00	45,00	1850,00

Table 16.3 How much annual staff time in hours would you say that your library staff expends in teaching faculty about publication lists and rankings, citation impact tools and methods, and other bibliometrics and citation analysis processes and procedures? (One person working full time would be about 1850 hours) Broken out by Type of College

Type of College	Mean	Median	Minimum	Maximum
Public	393,32	90,00	0,00	1850,00
Private	87,50	62,50	25,00	200,00

Table 16.4 How much annual staff time in hours would you say that your library staff expends in teaching faculty about publication lists and rankings, citation impact tools and methods, and other bibliometrics and citation analysis processes and procedures? (One person working full time would be about 1850 hours) Broken out by Annual Tuition Level

Annual Tuition Level	Mean	Median	Minimum	Maximum
less than $9000	256,67	45,00	0,00	1850,00
$9000 - $14000	732,88	596,50	15,00	1850,00
more than $14000	92,22	100,00	20,00	200,00

Table 16.5 How much annual staff time in hours would you say that your library staff expends in teaching faculty about publication lists and rankings, citation impact tools and methods, and other bibliometrics and citation analysis processes and procedures? (One person working full time would be about 1850 hours) Broken out by FTE Student Enrollment

FTE Student Enrollment	Mean	Median	Minimum	Maximum
less than 11000	386,36	50,00	10,00	1850,00
11000 - 22000	133,75	65,00	0,00	500,00
more than 22000	526,14	100,00	0,00	1850,00

Table 16.6 How much annual staff time in hours would you say that your library staff expends in teaching faculty about publication lists and rankings, citation impact tools and methods, and other bibliometrics and citation analysis processes and procedures? (One person working full time would be about 1850 hours) Broken out by Carnegie Class

Carnegie Class	Mean	Median	Minimum	Maximum
4-Year College	285,00	100,00	40,00	900,00
MA/PHD Granting	89,17	62,50	0,00	200,00
Research University	458,00	75,00	0,00	1850,00

Table 17 Does the library produce any of the following bibliometrics reports?

Table 17.1.1 Does the library produce ad hoc bibliometrics reports when requested by faculty or administration?

	No Answer	Yes	No
Entire sample	0,00%	64,52%	35,48%

Table 17.1.2 Does the library produce ad hoc bibliometrics reports when requested by faculty or administration? Broken out by Country

Country	Yes	No
USA	58,33%	41,67%
UK / Ireland	90,00%	10,00%
All Other	44,44%	55,56%

Table 17.1.3 Does the library produce ad hoc bibliometrics reports when requested by faculty or administration? Broken out by Type of College

Type of College	Yes	No
Public	66,67%	33,33%
Private	50,00%	50,00%

Table 17.1.4 Does the library produce ad hoc bibliometrics reports when requested by faculty or administration? Broken out by Annual Tuition Level

Annual Tuition Level	Yes	No
less than $9000	45,45%	54,55%
$9000 - $14000	80,00%	20,00%
more than $14000	70,00%	30,00%

Table 17.1.5 Does the library produce ad hoc bibliometrics reports when requested by faculty or administration? Broken out by FTE Student Enrollment

FTE Student Enrollment	Yes	No
less than 11000	90,91%	9,09%
11000 - 22000	50,00%	50,00%
more than 22000	50,00%	50,00%

Table 17.1.6 Does the library produce ad hoc bibliometrics reports when requested by faculty or administration? Broken out by Carnegie Class

Carnegie Class	Yes	No
4-Year College	25,00%	75,00%
MA/PHD Granting	33,33%	66,67%
Research University	88,89%	11,11%

Table 17.2.1 Does the library produce reports in specific fields produced at regular and expected intervals?

	No Answer	Yes	No
Entire sample	0,00%	25,81%	74,19%

Table 17.2.2 Does the library produce reports in specific fields produced at regular and expected intervals? Broken out by Country

Country	Yes	No
USA	25,00%	75,00%
UK / Ireland	30,00%	70,00%
All Other	22,22%	77,78%

Table 17.2.3 Does the library produce reports in specific fields produced at regular and expected intervals? Broken out by Type of College

Type of College	Yes	No
Public	25,93%	74,07%
Private	25,00%	75,00%

Table 17.2.4 Does the library produce reports in specific fields produced at regular and expected intervals? Broken out by Annual Tuition Level

Annual Tuition Level	Yes	No
less than $9000	27,27%	72,73%
$9000 - $14000	20,00%	80,00%
more than $14000	30,00%	70,00%

Table 17.2.5 Does the library produce reports in specific fields produced at regular and expected intervals? Broken out by FTE Student Enrollment

FTE Student Enrollment	Yes	No
less than 11000	45,45%	54,55%
11000 - 22000	20,00%	80,00%
more than 22000	10,00%	90,00%

Table 17.2.6 Does the library produce reports in specific fields produced at regular and expected intervals? Broken out by Carnegie Class

Carnegie Class	Yes	No
4-Year College	25,00%	75,00%
MA/PHD Granting	0,00%	100,00%
Research University	38,89%	61,11%

Table 17.3.1 Does the library produce bibliometrics reports about scholarly output of library personnel or faculty?

	No Answer	Yes	No
Entire sample	0,00%	22,58%	77,42%

Table 17.3.2 Does the library produce bibliometrics reports about scholarly output of library personnel or faculty? Broken out by Country

Country	Yes	No
USA	8,33%	91,67%
UK / Ireland	30,00%	70,00%
All Other	33,33%	66,67%

Table 17.3.3 Does the library produce bibliometrics reports about scholarly output of library personnel or faculty? Broken out by Type of College

Type of College	Yes	No
Public	25,93%	74,07%
Private	0,00%	100,00%

Table 17.3.4 Does the library produce bibliometrics reports about scholarly output of library personnel or faculty? Broken out by Annual Tuition Level

Annual Tuition Level	Yes	No
less than $9000	18,18%	81,82%
$9000 - $14000	20,00%	80,00%
more than $14000	30,00%	70,00%

Table 17.3.5 Does the library produce bibliometrics reports about scholarly output of library personnel or faculty? Broken out by FTE Student Enrollment

FTE Student Enrollment	Yes	No
less than 11000	18,18%	81,82%
11000 - 22000	30,00%	70,00%
more than 22000	20,00%	80,00%

Table 17.3.6 Does the library produce bibliometrics reports about scholarly output of library personnel or faculty? Broken out by Carnegie Class

Carnegie Class	Yes	No
4-Year College	0,00%	100,00%
MA/PHD Granting	11,11%	88,89%
Research University	33,33%	66,67%

All forms of bibliometrics analysis have some limitations. Some citations of an article may point out that the article is unexceptional or erroneous; major bibliometrics tools indices only cover a certain range of publications, etc. and may create a misleading picture. Has your library devised a "cocktail" or master formula to minimize the disadvantages of any one approach and to insure breadth and reliability, at least to the extent that this is possible. If so describe the methodologies that your library has developed. (Also identify yourself if you wish for this question).

1) based on all the 'none's' above, NO
2) No
3) No
4) No
5) No.
6) No
7) I think the general rule is use at least three indicators, never rely on just one.
8) No
9) We explain these issues but only in conversation. We don't have a structured or specified way to explain these topics.
10) We're not that far along yet.
11) The methodology is confined to a single data set: WoS.
12) We provide advanced bibliometrics indicators. Although not entirely, they try to cancel out and oddities mentioned, by benchmarking against world baselines.
13) I would check citation counts on: Web of Science, Scopus Google Scholar / Publish or Perish. Check for altmetrics for publications with Altmetric.com Check for downloads for publications on our institutional repository
14) No
15) We are aware of the shortcomings of the tools and ensure that we include a range of metrics from various sources and explain the problems with each.
16) We do not have that; but an explanation is made for each case.
17) n/a
18) No. We advise users but no more
19) No - we try to increase awareness of the products and issues, but leave methodological decisions up to the faculty member.
20) no, not to my knowledge
21) No, we have no master formula but one would be very helpful.
22) None.

23) In my research I try to do a broad analysis using various citation managers to give my research depth and breadth
24) Major advice given is never to place too much reliance on a single bibliometrics measure. No master formulas developed.

Table 18.1 Has the library been asked to participate in studies through which a kind of scholarly output "return on investment" might be calculated by comparing dollars invested in research to the resulting scholarly output?

	No Answer	Yes	No
Entire sample	12,90%	0,00%	87,10%

If you have participated in any studies through which the link between sums of money or time invested and scholarly output are linked then please describe one of these projects.

1) personal work/too extensive to describe
2) No
3) No
4) None
5) N/A
6) Similar analyses run but not involving comparisons with research investment / grant income

Table 19.1 Does the library manage a bibliometrics database that periodically measures the likely impact of publications from the college's faculty?

	No Answer	Yes	No
Entire sample	12,90%	6,45%	80,65%

Table 19.2 Does the library manage a bibliometrics database that periodically measures the likely impact of publications from the college's faculty? Broken out by Country

Country	No Answer	Yes	No
USA	0,00%	0,00%	100,00%
UK / Ireland	10,00%	10,00%	80,00%
All Other	33,33%	11,11%	55,56%

Table 19.3 Does the library manage a bibliometrics database that periodically measures the likely impact of publications from the college's faculty? Broken out by Type of College

Type of College	No Answer	Yes	No
Public	14,81%	7,41%	77,78%
Private	0,00%	0,00%	100,00%

Table 19.4 Does the library manage a bibliometrics database that periodically measures the likely impact of publications from the college's faculty? Broken out by Annual Tuition Level

Annual Tuition Level	No Answer	Yes	No
less than $9000	18,18%	9,09%	72,73%
$9000 - $14000	0,00%	10,00%	90,00%
more than $14000	20,00%	0,00%	80,00%

Table 19.5 Does the library manage a bibliometrics database that periodically measures the likely impact of publications from the college's faculty? Broken out by FTE Student Enrollment

FTE Student Enrollment	No Answer	Yes	No
less than 11000	0,00%	9,09%	90,91%
11000 - 22000	10,00%	10,00%	80,00%
more than 22000	30,00%	0,00%	70,00%

Table 19.6 Does the library manage a bibliometrics database that periodically measures the likely impact of publications from the college's faculty? Broken out by Carnegie Class

Carnegie Class	No Answer	Yes	No
4-Year College	0,00%	0,00%	100,00%
MA/PHD Granting	11,11%	0,00%	88,89%
Research University	16,67%	11,11%	72,22%

If yes how controversial is this database in your institution? What are the politics involved in challenging it? Is there some form of appeal mechanism?

1) Considering symplectic elements - not sure what reception will be among faculty. Administrators seem to be interested in it.
2) It is currently virtually unused - this is about to change however.
3) Neither
4) Our research office manages this role. Issues that I know of are (1) many researchers do not feel that benchmarking their research against others in their School/College is appropriate because e.g. their specific area of research is poorly cited and (2) the average or median benchmarks create a lot of stress for researchers in high achieving Schools / Colleges because many that fall below these metrics are still doing quite well by national and international standards.
5) We just bought InCites ... or rather one of the colleges at our University has done so. Based on what I've seen so far, the results are incomplete and misleading.
6) You need to discuss and explain this all the time and every time. But after 10 years' experience they have become adjusted to this, and we have built considerable experience with having this discussion. Mind you 85% of our university is in the Life sciences, so that makes is more acceptable.
7) NA
8) N/A
9) Have run such a database previously but now discontinued

How does the library promote its bibliometrics and citation analysis services?

1) has nothing to promote
2) Run regular training via Staff Development Dept., but not otherwise promoted as little staff time to devote to it.
3) Intranet page
4) We don't.
5) It doesn't
6) through orientations, targeted emails, and training sessions (group and on-on-one)
7) Web pages, one to ones, training sessions, emails.
8) Leaflets, reports, ..
9) We don't offer any services other than skilling researchers to analyse/manage their own bibliometrics and citation performance. This is promoted in presentations, one-on-one meetings, casual conversations, etc.
10) We don't yet. I have started working on a LibGuide and plan to offer short training sessions.
11) training seminars and outreach programme, open access argument, metrics used in the context of demonstrating impact
12) I do it! Currently fairly ad hoc. Some training available from academic librarians
13) Via the research office.
14) Newsletters, yearly evaluations cycles etc.
15) Via an email list Via Twitter and Library Blog Via LCD Screen in Library building At workshops On website Speaking at faculty board meetings and other invited forums
16) Through subject librarian liaison
17) Via website, word of mouth, workshops, attendance at seminars
18) We have a group of subject specialist, each does their own promotion - but it is minimum
19) not yet but within the next year
20) Through research workshops
21) By training and web page.
22) mostly by individual subject liaisons
23) Through library training programmes and by referrals from the institution's research and postgraduate support directorate
24) Talking with faculty
25) Through workshops and liaison activities as well as the marketing departments communication schedule
26) Internal e-mails and blogs

What advice can you offer to your peers on the best way to establish, promote and manage a bibliometrics service at their college or university?

1) Learn the tools. Benefits obvious.
2) Provide high quality reports to administrators so that they see the value of it.
3) Most successful when it is scientist to scientist.
4) Try and get a Bibliometrician if you can!
5) obtain the necessary skills and knowledge and then tell your manager about the problems associate with bibliometrics analysis provided by unskilled
6) I'm going to have more extensive talks with our Dean first. We do plan to have one expert that improves the overall knowledge of all subject librarians.
7) Involve library/information/metrics staff with academics and departments. Make sure all staff are aware of developments in this area. Offer regular training/update information. Be visible.
8) Do not confine analysis to a single data set. Explore alt-metrics. Improve repository statistics.
9) http://www.slideshare.net/Wowter/bibliometrics-in-the-library
10) Get training yourself in bibliometrics, attend the European Summer School for Scientometrics. Talk to people in other libraries that have establish a similar service. Meet and talk with other relevant offices and people on campus. Promote the service as in answer 31.
11) We have very little experience
12) Be very familiar with the tools and their limitations. Keep on top of developments both in terms of new metrics and changes in tools
13) It's a good idea; I will explore this topic with my supervisors to see how we can do it.
14) think in terms of disciplinarity specific use cases (i.e. humanities are less interested in altmetrics), and teach with people stories rather than about just the tools when you're starting from the ground up
15) Work with interested staff in departments to evangelise
16) There's an upcoming book from ACRL Press designed to help familiarize librarians with bibliometrics and altmetrics, along with what libraries are doing to help support these services, so I advise that they read it when it comes out! (I'm the co-author of this book ...)
17) Promoting bibliometrics services from the library when academic staff need it.
18) alerting faculty that the service is available, what it does, and what such analyses can and cannot accomplish
19) We have started small and hope to grow this service as our Doctoral programs expand and the research output of our institution develops
20) Do it, talk about it, present results at internal and external conferences and meetings. Show the numbers and how there is ROI
21) Spend regular time with your faculty academics each week, discussing research at a general level. Your expertise will then become known and requests start to come in by word-of-mouth